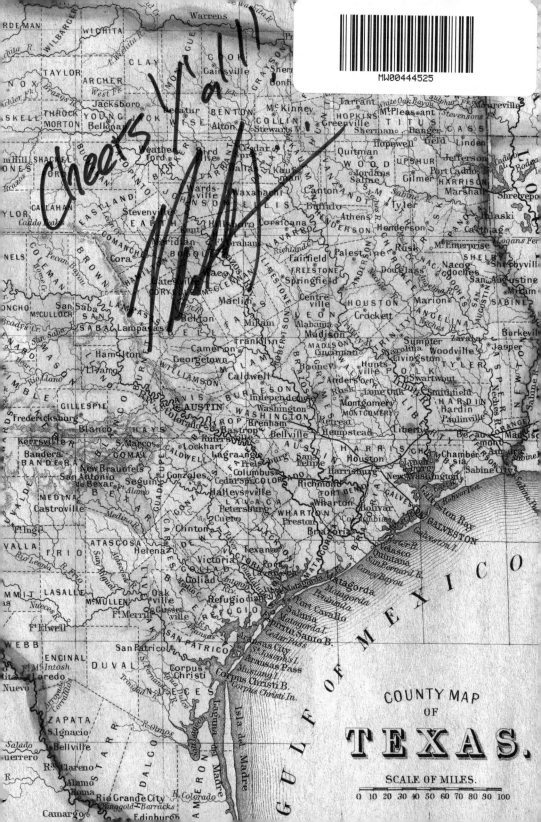

COUNTY MAP
OF

TEXAS.

SCALE OF MILES.

0 10 20 30 40 50 60 70 80 90 100

TEXAS
WHISKEY

TEXAS

WHISKEY

WORLD-CLASS BOURBONS, PREMIER RYES, AND NEW SINGLE MALTS FROM THE LONE STAR STATE

PHOTOGRAPHY BY
~ JOHN WHALEN ~

~ NICO MARTINI ~

CIDER MILL
PRESS

BOOK
PUBLISHERS
KENNEBUNKPORT, MAINE

CONTENTS

INTRODUCTION ★

INTRODUCTION

JOHN GUNTER SAID, "If a man's from Texas, he'll tell you. If he's not, why embarrass him by asking?" Sure, every state in the union has its individual identity, but Texas is just a little more vainglorious. There's even a Wikipedia entry for "Texas Pride."

Swagger is one thing we have in spades. What can I say? We're obnoxious but charming. We're brazen and perfectly happy to tell you all about it, or just quietly let you figure it out for yourself, because we're also the nicest people you'll ever meet. Our mamas taught us right and while we generally consider ourselves tough SOBs, we're also respectful as all get out. There have been honest-to-goodness academic studies dedicated to deciphering Texas braggadocio. It makes sense. I'm pretty sure we start learning Texas history in third grade and keep it up well into junior high.

Some of the studies specifically point to the Battle of the Alamo as the major event that kicked our Texas pride into full gear. William Travis, line in the sand, one of us for every twenty of them, blah, blah, just go watch the movie. "Remember the Alamo" became our battle cry. Then we won and there was much rejoicing. We're the only state that used to be its own country and if we felt like it, could split into five different states. Y'all realize that Texas is the size of Spain, right? Inside our borders, you could fit three Kentuckys, two Tennessees, and still have room for Florida. Hell, the DFW Airport is the size of Manhattan. Everything's bigger because we have the room to do it. Texas goes big.

The Texas Highway Department knew this in 1985, when it started the Don't Mess with Texas campaign to reduce littering. It's the Texas mindset and the Texas pride that make such a phrase become part of our vernacular, which is also known the world over. Damn right, you better not mess with Texas. In fact, the federal government does not own any land in Texas and we also must approve any action the federal government wishes to take on Texas land. The whole flying our flag the same height as the American flag thing is pretty sweet too.

We're polite, we're friendly, we're constantly helping our neighbors, and we're more than happy to shut down our distilleries in the middle of a pandemic so we can retool everything to make hand sanitizer. In total, Texas distilleries have donated over $6 million in hand sanitizer to health care professionals and first responders. Helping our brothers and sisters will always be more important than money to a Texan. Truly.

We're a massive melting pot that somehow understands that even though this stew has a whole bunch of different parts, it only tastes good and it only works because everything blends together to create a completely unique flavor.

We understand that if we join forces, we can all be more successful, and that will allow us to create even stronger communities. And I say this knowing damn well how fiercely independent we are at the same time. Even those who move here and make Texas their home — you don't move to Texas, Texas moves into you.

T. R. Fehrenbach once said that Texas was "not a society but a people." Texans are a true amalgamation. When I was working on the book *Texas Cocktails*, I kept thinking about how much of a responsibility it was to document a story that had yet to be told. I did what any Texan would do and I asked for help. It turned into much less of "me" and much more of "y'all" because it wound up featuring over 100 different bars and bartenders and spirits makers and spirits purveyors and generally everyone I could find that would have something to say about the Texas cocktail scene and its remarkable growth. It's a snapshot of dozens of mini-stories, told through cocktail recipes and chitchat. But whiskey is a different beast entirely.

When I was working in theater as a director, I used a very simple approach to storytelling: you pick a good story, you pick the right actors, and you get the hell out of the way. The story of Texas whiskey is already one of the tallest of tales in the spirits world and the characters are often those around whom fables are built. This book shows you how steadfast we are when it comes to this story we're writing. I'll try to stay out of the way.

The first written mention of Scotch was in 1495 and noted that a friar named John Cor was the distiller at Lindores Abbey. The first record of Irish whiskey was ninety years prior. Japan's first commercial production of their version was in 1924, but whisky production began there around 1870. In the US, rye whiskey was first produced in the 1790s in Pennsylvania, with bourbon quickly following in Kentucky. Texas' first whiskey hit the market in 2008.

If we're this good at making whiskey now, just wait until we're twenty years in. See? Swagger, baby.

Texas whiskey: a little over a decade ago those words meant nothing. They didn't exist together as a thought. I can already tell you that my favorite part of this book is going to be updating it. The Texas whiskey industry is moving at breakneck speed and that's not because of the whiskey "aging faster" here. We are, literally, just getting started.

The Texas whiskey industry began with the inception of Garrison Brothers and Balcones. Dan Garrison started down his path by heading to Kentucky and soaking up every ounce of knowledge he could get from some of the most famous whiskey makers in the history of bourbon. When he returned to Texas, he somehow managed to kick off the consulting career of the Johnny Appleseed of American whiskey, Dave Pickerell, and he started making his Texas bourbon. The thing is, he had no idea if this was going to work. He thought it would, and certainly hoped it would, but there were more variables here than you could shake a stick at. Texas whiskey was a gamble, make no bones about it, and this was a game for wildcatters.

Enter Chip Tate and the Balcones crew. Tate visited Garrison Brothers to poke around a bit and next thing you know, he's released the first Texas whiskey. So, for those who need this tidbit, here's the final answer. Garrison Brothers *made* the first Texas whiskey, which was aging when Tate paid his visit. Balcones *released* the first Texas whiskey, a five-week-old corn whiskey, in September 2009. What a delightfully "Texas" beginning to it all.

I can honestly say that before working on this book, I had no clue that industry legends like Pickerell and Nancy Fraley had their hands all over the Texas whiskey industry, laying the foundation for these magical elixirs we're making now. We truly started with the best, took their knowledge, and began to figure out how to make whiskey in this environment. Texas is unquestionably the most diverse whiskey region in the world today and a slew of distillers have joined the Texas whiskey scene, varying from those only making a thousand bottles of whiskey a year to those with the capacity to produce millions of gallons. But I'll be damned if we're not putting out some of the best whiskey on the planet from a whiskey region that's the age of an eighth grader.

The greatest thing the Texas whiskey industry has going for it is the utter lack of tradition. Collectively, we don't even know which kind of whiskey is going to be best suited for being produced in Texas. I know I had different thoughts about what I wanted to be when I grew up at the age of twelve than I did at twenty, and our little industry is similar. We value the legacy and the history of the whiskey makers that have come before us, and we've certainly absorbed their ideas to help

root ourselves in the ways of American whiskey, but, ultimately, we don't really care about traditions. In Texas, if we don't have traditions, we write our own.

Texas whiskey is creativity and innovation. We have the two largest distilleries west of the Mississippi and we have won just about every single award a whiskey or distillery can win. And, according to *Whisky Magazine*, we currently produce the world's best bourbon. Bourbon of the Year, Corn Whiskey of the Year, Distillery of the Year, Micro-Distillery of the Year, Craft Distillery of the Year, Master Distiller of the Year, and on and on. We're making some of the most creative and most lauded whiskey anywhere and we aren't even old enough to shave.

We have distilleries primarily focusing on technology and automation, we have mom and pop shops where literally everyone working there is related, we have folks that are reinventing the corn industry to create grain better suited for whiskey production, and, as of late, we have had multiple investments from some of the world's largest international spirits companies. We're making bourbon, rye, single malts, smoked single malts, blended bourbons, single malt finished in a cider barrel, rye made in part with triticale (a wheat and rye hybrid), and bourbons that have rice in their mash bill, straight malted ryes, wheat whiskey, whiskeys of various ages, light whiskey, sourced whiskey, whiskey that's sourced then blended here, whiskey that's sourced then aged here, grain-to-glass whiskey, Certified Texas Whiskey (see page 40) — you name it, we'll give it a go.

However, the Texas whiskey industry has been working through an identity crisis since its inception. As Spencer Whalen, Executive Director of the Texas Whiskey Association can attest, there has not always been the greatest transparency in our industry. We've had our fair share of folks buying whiskey from MGP or Dickel and throwing a Texas flag on a bottle shaped like cowboy boots (truth be told, I don't think that actually exists, and frankly, I might buy that, but I digress; I am Texan you know).

Since the outset, there has been a sourced whiskey problem. It feels like every time I walk down the whiskey aisle at my favorite big box liquor store there's some new and exciting straight bourbon whiskey "from" Texas named after a character in the TV show *Dallas* or some Texas river or trail. It seems like we're many years and many political lobbying dollars away from this changing, but the accidental benefit to this is the community that has developed around those trying to do something about it. Among distillers in Texas, you'll see camaraderie unlike anywhere else in the spirits industry.

The greatest thing about the sourced whiskey problem is that our distillers have had to team up to fight this battle. The enemy of our enemies are our friends. There's a sense of solidarity among our distillers and this has created not only an "us against the world" atmosphere, but it serves as the bedrock for some of the most interesting collaborations you'll find anywhere. I've seen three different distillers hand over barrels of whiskey to a blender, sight unseen, and allow them to create something new with them. This is not normal behavior for headstrong whiskey makers.

This collaborative spirit is not limited to distillers. Kris Hart, founder of the Houston Whiskey Social and host of the Whiskey Neat podcast, says that the reason for the Texas whiskey boom is because the distillers are willing to engage the consumer. The distillers here, for the most part, will work with anyone. This is a culture of "yes." This doesn't happen anywhere else. You can't get the big guys in Kentucky to do a third of the things the distillers here do. Hart told me about a project where they had a bourbon barrel and used it to make a bourbon-aged honey. Then they took that barrel, with about five gallons of honey left in it, and convinced Balcones to fill it with a single malt and set it to age. This is an example of the possibilities when there's a culture of collaboration, and the opportunities have just begun to scratch the surface. There's also going to be a massive expansion in blending and private labeling driven by these types of projects and distillers who are willing to do so.

Those in favor of transparency, we'll call "the good guys" and those who are not, we'll call "those lowlifes." Because of this surge in deceptive practices, the good guys have joined forces and are now engaged in a battle royale against those lowlifes who take up shelf space with their misleading labels. It's working, frankly. There's a movement within the state among consumers who have started to demand to know where their whiskey is coming from and those who can't say "our distillery, come by and see us" are inherently at a disadvantage. There are plenty of forces the good guys have to fight, including an archaic set of arbitrary laws from almost a century ago, and those who ultimately benefit from this system and fight like hell to keep it in place, and a state government that apparently doesn't value them. But, ultimately, these forces are the very things that have forced the good guys to work in solidarity. If you'd like a shortcut to those who are dedicated to 100% transparency and grain-to-glass whiskey, the Texas Whiskey Association is an incredible organization.

I'M WRITING THIS IN THE MIDDLE OF A PANDEMIC. When I went to visit some of these distilleries, I had to pass a COVID test before I was allowed on the property. This was not a good time to be joyriding from distillery to distillery. I should have been home, no matter how brief or socially distant the visits were, but I managed to visit everyone.

The Texas whiskey industry spent the second quarter of 2020 converting their operations to produce hand sanitizer. Collectively, the Texas whiskey industry gave away over $6 million in sanitizer to medical professionals and first responders, and they also weren't making any money at this time. They were told to shut down entirely. Later they were permitted to operate, but they couldn't open their tasting rooms.

Broadly speaking, craft distilleries are struggling, so friends, once there is a little more normalcy, please visit whichever distillery grabs you. I promise you'll have a great time visiting any distillery featured in the book. In my opinion, they were transparent and honest about their operation—they're the good guys.

Texas has between twelve and fourteen micro-climates and our weather is about as volatile it comes. It's always going to take some figuring out. The Gulf Coast has seen years where the proof of an aging distillate didn't change because of the sheer amount of humidity in the air, and then there are Hill Country distilleries that lose damn near 20% a year to the angels. The climate differences in Texas are ridiculous. This place is absurd. Why in the world would you want to make whiskey here? Don't answer that. I'm just glad they are.

One thing that we should discuss, however, is the misconception that whiskey ages faster in Texas because of the temperature swings. Unless Doc Brown has started using the DeLorean as a rickhouse, you cannot speed up time. That's why the odds that you'll ever (yes, ever) see a Texas whiskey that's ten years old are slim. It may happen, but the Texas sweet spot is always going to be much younger than other whiskey-making regions. That being said, Texans have found ways to alter the rate in which the barrel impacts the liquid inside. Some use larger barrels, some use smaller barrels, some use élevage — a French word for how the final flavor of wine can be shaped between fermentation and bottling through barrel aging, filtering, and fining — some proof in barrel, but all of them know this is one of the biggest reasons the whiskey in Texas delivers such a punch. Plenty of the whiskey makers here love that punch, others are doing their damnedest to reduce it, but all of them are experimenting with ways to change their outcomes. Let's call it puberty.

Of note, one of the greatest contributions to Texas whiskey has been a focus on local grains. We have some incredible farmland in this state and it's amazing to see portions of it becoming dedicated to distillers. It's no surprise that some of the most impressive agricultural advancements specifically for the production of spirits are, and will come, from Texas. We have whiskey makers saving heirloom corn varietals from extinction and others literally growing their own wheat. Texas is responsible for some of the most inventive approaches to sustainability in this industry and there's more coming down the pike.

At some point in this intro, I'm supposed to talk about the history of Texas whiskey, but you should probably check back in about ten years. We'll still be making amazing whiskey, but we might just have a clue as to which ones work best, how to tame our heat and lack of humidity (except for those places that have it in abundance), and which grains our farmers are going to home in on so that we can be producing entirely homegrown products. I'd like to tell you about the history of Texas whiskey, but I can't. It's not ready. You're going to have to give me a couple of more editions worth of updates to get to the point where I'll feel comfortable calling anything here "our history."

This isn't Kentucky and we've never tried to be. This isn't Scotland, and while we love them, we have our own ideas about single malts, thank you very much. We don't have the weather consistency of an Ireland, and we don't really get seasons or adhere to specific ways of filtering like Tennessee. Honestly, I hope this book serves as the first documentation of our whiskey history. But for now, this is a portrait of a twelve-year-old industry. I look forward to reading the first real book about the "history" of Texas whiskey in a couple of decades and, god willing, I'll be available if anyone needs a quote from an old timer who was just trying to let the story tell itself. The same as Jared Himstedt at Balcones is a little uncomfortable with the idea of being declared a master distiller, I'm a bit uncomfortable with anything about an industry so young and so rapidly changing being referred to as "history." We'll get there.

For now, I offer a thorough look at the present, letting those in this industry have the opportunity to use their own words to explain to you how and why they do what they do, from Spencer Whelan arguing for massive bureaucratic over-hauls to all of the current code to Blaze May breaking down the malting process and Daniel Whittington explaining the need and the value of independent bottling companies. As the story progresses, I'll do my best to keep on top of it at my site — texaswhiskeybook.com — because since the day I turned this sucker in, more history has been written.

We stand on the precipice of greatness. There's so much more to come from this story and without any of those nettlesome traditions to hold us down, we'll be able to push the envelope for decades to come. The Texas whiskey industry is trying every technique imaginable to figure out what Texas whiskey should truly be. The Texas whiskey industry already has a lot to be proud of, but we also know there's work to be done. If you don't think we're the best, you will soon enough, and if you don't, well bless your heart!

TASTE THE TRUTH

HOW CERTIFIED TEXAS WHISKEY
DRAWS A LINE IN THE SAND

SPENCER WHELAN

"Remember the Alamo!"
"The Eyes of Texas Are Upon You!"
"Don't Mess With Texas!"

Whether you are a Texan or not, you have likely heard these phrases and know them to be part of the state's heritage. They are the rallying cries of Texans past who staked a claim on the grounds of independence, autonomy, and personal accountability. These words echo through the generations, and to this day, strike a chord in the hearts of every man, woman, and child who looks admirably at the Lone Star flag. They are also great advertising slogans.

That's the dichotomy of Texas. A state forged in part by legitimacy and in part by legend. A state vast and diverse, yet singular in its reputation. Go almost any-where in the world and show someone the shape of the border lines of the state and there's a greater than likely chance they will exclaim, "Texas!" Start singing the phrase, "The stars at night, are big and bright..." and chances are the people around you will clap four times in quick succession then wait in anticipation for you to join them in a chorus of, "Deep in the heart of Texas!" In short, Texas has some top-notch brand awareness.

What does this have to do with whiskey? Well, anyone who knows anything about the whiskey industry knows that to sell a whiskey product, you need to be at least as good of a marketer as you are a whiskey maker. To put it into terms Texans can understand, if whiskey was a game of Texas football the "brand" would be playing QB, calling the plays, reading the field, and speaking at the pep-rally to get fans' butts in the seats. The whiskey in the bottle would be playing on the line, protecting the brand from assault and steadily making progress down the field— ensuring everything comes together to defeat their fiercest rivals. To continue the metaphor, some whiskey companies build their teams around the exciting transfer star QB from out of town who slings the ball around the field and puts points on the board. Meanwhile, others will slowly build from within, focusing on fundamentals, perfecting their process, and cultivating talent until they are a cohesive force to be reckoned with. Over the last fourteen years, the Texas whiskey industry has seen its fair share of both strategies employed. However, one strategy put points on the board early and often.

If you listen in to Texans talking about someone else and they drop the "all hat and no cattle" descriptor — then you were a firsthand witness to a murder by words. In Texas, this means that the person in question has all the trappings of a wealthy and successful cattle rancher — new boots, pristine felt hat, perhaps a new crew-cab pickup — but clearly he's never rolled through a steaming pile of manure while wrestling a steer to the ground.

The early days of Texas whiskey have very much been a story of brands coming to market with all hat and no cattle. We've established that Texas has really good branding. So, when craft whiskey (specifically bourbon) began to boom in the mid 2000s, crafty marketers created a formula consisting of sourcing whiskey from places like Indiana, Kentucky, and Canada, and throwing Texas iconography all over the bottles. In many cases, the only thing "Texan" about these brands was the address of the holding company or bottling operation. The Department of Treasury's Tax and Trade Bureau does have regulations on the books to prevent this kind of deceptive marketing practice, but the ills of a large government bureaucracy combined with the onslaught of thousands of craft label submissions for approval meant that most of these protections were completely ineffective. The words "produced by," "bottled by," and "crafted by" replaced the more transparent "distilled by" qualifier set before the company's location statement on bottles.

Some brands literally draped their bottles in the Texas flag hoping that enough state pride would blind the consumer to the fact that the most time that whiskey had spent in Texas was the time it spent on the shelves of a Texas package store. And it worked.

While these early "Texas whiskey" brands enjoyed the early spotlight and the comfortable revenue, other distillers were busy experimenting with their first batches of bourbon, corn whiskey, rye, and single malts. They were working out little problems: like how to keep the barrels from exploding in the scorching Texas summer heat; or, if you can keep the wood intact, how to prevent a "ghost barrel"

where almost all the liquid is lost to evaporation; and, if you can harvest enough barrels, how do you make sure the product actually tastes good? It is a dance in which a distiller or blender must take the hand of their partner environment and learn the steps together. As Jared Himstedt of Balcones Distilling says, "It took us ten years to understand the kind of whiskey Texas wants us to make."

THE FOUR Ts

Bourbon from Kentucky isn't the amazing American spirit we know today without the hard-earned knowledge of bourbon-making—taking sweet American corn mashed with other heartland grains and mineral-rich water, then distilling them into a new charred oak barrel. Scotch whisky isn't a premium product without years of soul-stretching trial and error, experimenting with local ingredients, dealing with local weather conditions, and cultivating talented stewards to pass down the knowledge of their craft through the generations. These great whiskey regions of the world have all achieved mastery of "the Four Ts": Terroir, Time, Talent, Truth.

"Terroir" is a term shamelessly stolen from wine-making but is also applicable to whiskey. It is the environmental conditions (soil impacts on base grains, temperatures, barometric pressure, humidity, etc.) that directly impact the taste of the whiskey. Scotch whisky has five distinct regions where the terroir of the regions helps determine the style of the end product. All five of those regions can fit into a land mass roughly the size of the "Texas Triangle"—the space inside an invisible polygon drawn between Dallas-Fort Worth, Houston, San Antonio, and Austin. How many regions of Texas whiskey will develop their own "terroir"? So far we've identified at least four regions based on climate and maturation conditions, but as the industry grows we eagerly anticipate what is possible as more whiskey pioneers explore the vast terroir of Texas.

"Time" is self-evident. It takes time to make a great whiskey. In Texas it takes considerably less time to age a whiskey because of the extreme climate conditions throughout the state. Highly volatile temperature and pressure changes push the whiskey in and out of the wood at a higher frequency than most places on earth. It turbo-charges the maturation process, but it doesn't come without cost. Angel's share (evaporation loss in the barrel) in a place like Scotland can be around .5-2%

of the total barrel volume. A year of aging in Texas can net you a 18-20% loss of the barrel. In other words, the angels are thirstier in Texas and time is as much adversary as it is an ally to whiskey makers.

"Talent" is the skill needed to tame the feral Texas whiskey into a unique expression that imparts that "sense of place" when it hits your palate. The compressed time-frame of maturation in Texas also means there is significantly more human interaction with the products. In Scotland, a barrel may remain sealed for several years before regular sampling. The same is true, but with more frequency, in making Kentucky bourbon. In Texas, a blender may need to be sampling the barrels as quickly as a couple of months after entry into the barrel. When prepping a barrel for harvesting (dumping) a distiller/blender may be checking on it daily to ensure that the latest cold front hasn't squeezed too much whiskey out of the wood too fast, resulting in a whiskey that tastes like chewing on a charred barrel stave. Miss your window, and you may need to wait until the temperature rises and stabilizes long enough to push those acrid flavors back into the wood. In other parts of the whiskey world, you are tasting the generational work of distillers and blenders past who likely couldn't see their own products come to fruition. In Texas, when you taste a quality whiskey, you are tasting the talents of contemporary men and women who are accountable for their own products in near real time.

"Truth" is well...the truth. It's the credibility needed in a premium whiskey so the consumer knows they can trust how it was made. Make no mistake, alcohol products can be dangerous both in the way they are consumed and in the way they are made. Anyone who cares about what they put into their body should care to know the who, what, when, and where of a product to ensure that it is safe. Ensuring the intrinsic consumer safety in a distilled spirit is the duty of distillers and regulators, but gaining the trust of consumers is the duty of marketers and storytellers. Texas whiskey has been hamstrung by years of misleading marketing that capitalized on the branding of our state without putting the terroir, time, and talent into the well-branded bottle itself. While some of these early brands reinvested their success into building a true Texas-based whiskey practice, many others did not, and consumers became wise to the deception. As a result, the truth needed an advocate. Enter the Texas Whiskey Association.

We created the Texas Whiskey Association and our Certified Texas Whiskey standards to educate and tell the story of these amazing whiskey makers in order to give consumers a simple mark of quality that they can trust. We defined Certified Texas Whiskey (CTW) as simply any whiskey product in which all five core steps of the whiskey-making process—mashing, fermentation, distillation, maturation, bottling—all occur within the territorial boundaries of Texas. This gives freedom to the distillers to innovate with grains, methods, barrels, and maturation styles from around the world while ensuring an industry where makers, not just marketers and bottlers, come to Texas to plant roots. We then certify these processes every year by visiting the distilleries and ensuring all five steps are in fact being done at a scale matching their reported output for certified products.

Next, we created the Certified Native Texas Whiskey standard, which takes all the standards of a CTW product and adds the following requirements: all the grains must be harvested from Texas; it must be produced entirely at a single distillery in Texas; it must be aged a minimum of twenty-four months; it must be unadulterated with any flavoring, coloring, or blending materials. This standard will ensure the Texas whiskey industry achieves the goal of growing supporting industries like Texas farmers, and seed producers, and malters. It establishes a level of accountability for both the whiskey maker and consumer, allowing them to forge trust and learn from each other. To put it simply, it creates a truth you can taste.

So when we say "Taste The Truth," yes it is a memorable piece of marketing and, yes, it is a battle cry for all consumers of true Texas whiskey. However, what we are really trying to achieve is the creation of an environment where the legend of Texas whiskey is based on legitimacy, accountability, and independence of spirit. We know that road is long and we are just getting started. But, in a world where it seems like pretense and manipulation infect all aspects of our lives, let's start with truth.

Spencer Whelan is the Executive Director of the Texas Whiskey Association, an organization dedicated to the fight for transparency and accountability in the Texas whiskey industry.

CERTIFIED TEXAS WHISKEY

The Texas Whiskey Association was created as a direct response to some of the sourcing practices of so-called Texas whiskeys that are primarily sourced whiskey from outside the state and marketed with the intention of making the consumer think they're from here. Now, while sourcing itself is not inherently evil, throwing a Texas flag or some boots on a label or naming yourself after some sort of nature something or other located in Texas and calling yourself a Texas whiskey is awfully shady. I've done my best to not include any of these shady whiskeys in this book. The Texas Whiskey Association couldn't possibly have any of them in their organization because of their vetting process.

In order to be a Certified Texas Whiskey, according to their website, the standards that must be met are:

1. Produced at licensed distilleries wholly located within the State of Texas.

2. Produced from cereal grains (whole grain, ground grain, or grain flakes) and Texas-sourced water that is...

   - Processed in the state of Texas into a mash

   - Fermented entirely in the state of Texas

   - Distilled and barreled in the State of Texas

   - Compliant with the TTB designations of "Whisk(e)y" both in class & type

3. Matured entirely within the territorial boundaries of the State of Texas.

4. Bottled within the State of Texas with no additives other than Texas-sourced water.

5. Independently verified via on-site annual verification by an officer of The Texas Whiskey Association compliance team.

The Texas Whiskey Association was created by Spencer Whelan. "Because I worked in public affairs, I saw what was happening in the Texas wine industry. It boomed, but the reputation started to decline because of a lack of transparency. There was a lot of California and Oregon wine being sold as Texas wine," Whelan said. "It's so important to protect the identity of Texas because Texas is an international brand. The flag, the shape, the name all have a brand that's known and it's a great marketing opportunity. The easiest thing to do is to take advantage of the brand without paying attention to the quality or the terroir or just the essence of what Texas is. The whiskeys being made in Texas are completely unique and completely distinct from the rest of the world."

Whelan and the team also create some of the most useful content on the internet when it comes to Texas whiskey. I can't tell you how helpful their YouTube channel has been throughout this process; some of my favorite interviews with the distillers in Texas have been done by Whelan and his wife Sarah.

The identity of Texas may be hard to pin down, but we know what we ain't. The Texas Whiskey Association fights to keep the spirit of Texas (get it?) in the whiskeys of Texas. This is a service to you, my friend, the consumer. "The Certified Texas Whiskey program is an effort to help consumers understand which products are from Texas and which are not. We're always going to air on the side of transparency for the consumer, because that's better for the consumer and for the Texas industry as a whole, namely because I think that the brand of Texas is too precious of an asset to the whiskey world to allow it to be diluted by products that are dishonest," Whelan told me.

NORTH TEXAS ★

NORTH TEXAS

NORTH TEXAS IS MY HOOD. Born and raised in Fort Worth, went to school in Plano and Denton, and currently living in Dallas. If you're around, let me know. I'm easy to find. One of my favorite things about this area is the mishmash of cultures, from the almost sickeningly modern atmosphere of Dallas, to the "this is what Austin was like back in the day, man" vibes of Denton, to the gateway of the West in Fort Worth, North Texas has everything you could hope for in an urban whiskey region. Except scenery. It's flat and boring, and while I love it... totally flat and very boring. Now, the distilleries, on the other hand, are quite the opposite. Ever had a single barrel bourbon made from scarce heirloom corn that has been aged on the same land that brought us Ben Hogan and Byron Nelson? Welcome to North Texas.

ACRE DISTILLING

HISTORICALLY, HELL'S HALF ACRE IN FORT WORTH was known as the most notoriously unruly of any Wild West red light district. Organized brawls, gambling, cockfighting, horse racing, and prostitution were all regular activities, and that was just on the weekdays. In 1881, a paper in Fort Worth said the area sprawled across 2 ½ acres and it was the first thing that trail drivers saw when approaching from the south. Known as "The Acre" to locals, Hell's Half Acre lived up to its reputation well into the 1920s. Today, the area is primarily taken up with a convention center that hosted the likes of my high school graduation and that Pantera New Year's Eve show where I lost a contact in the mosh pit. I guess one way to eliminate a sordid past is to plop a building on top of the entire area.

Tony Formby, owner of Acre Distilling, named after the old neighborhood, was a majority stakeholder in Rahr & Sons Brewing. When Formby sold his portion of the company, head brewer for Rahr & Sons, JB Flowers, along with his colleague, Brad Berven, decided they wanted to become distillers and make a slew of interesting whiskeys. They convinced Formby to invest and Acre Distilling was born.

Acre Distilling pays tribute to a host of the characters from Hell's Half Acre lore. Their bourbon is named after Longhair Jim Courtright, a lawman turned bad guy who was killed in an honest to goodness face-to-face shootout. Their gin is called Two Minnie's after a saloon of the same name, and Texas Jack, their peach-flavored whiskey, is named after Doc Middleton, a teenage horse thief turned lawman.

Acre Distilling has one of the most diverse product lines in Texas. They're currently sourcing their bourbons, but all of their flavored whiskeys, malt whiskeys, and their Hop Along Cassidy, a very cool collaboration with Rabbit Hole Brewery, are 100% Texas grain to glass. Of note, their Texas Single Malt took silver in the San Francisco World Spirits Competition and Acre Distilling was named the 2020 U.S. Open Spirits' Grand National Champion.

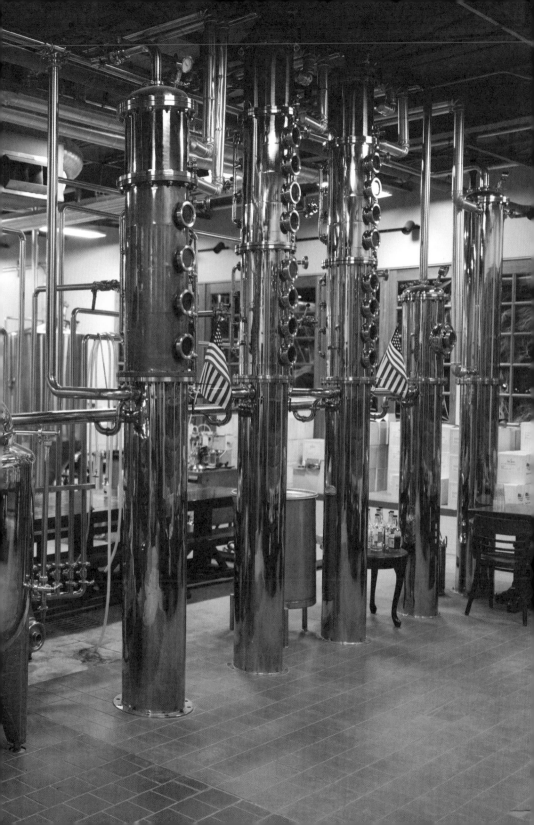

ACRE SINGLE MALT

Distilled from Texas barley, cold smoked over peach and pecan wood; 40% smoked malt, 60% malted barley.

PROOF: 100

NOSE: Cherry filling, Band-Aids, creosote, raspberry salad dressing.

PALATE: Dark chocolate-covered cherries, toasted marshmallow, old vine zinfandel on the long finish.

SMOKED SINGLE MALT

100% two-row barley from Hillsboro aged in 30-gallon, #3 char new American oak barrels.

PROOF: 100

NOSE: Charcoal outdoor grill, mushroom soup, overly oaky chardonnay, charred bell peppers.

PALATE: Musty, incense, light roast coffee, burnt sticks, Italian wedding cake, and I feel like I'm taking crazy pills but it tastes like Sotol on the finish.

BLACKLAND DISTILLERY

BLACKLAND DISTILLERY FEELS LIKE THE DISTILLERY that would be in a movie about some sort of dystopian future. Like many other craft distilleries, you can find Blackland in the middle of a major city, Fort Worth, down the street from the entertainment district, West 7th, situated in an industrial business park next to a record store and not far from the coffee shop/co-working space, no less. When you arrive, you pass through a modish, contemporary patio and into the upscale cocktail lounge. In fact, the tasting room is so swank that it took home the Bar of the Year award from a couple of local media outlets.

Markus Kypreos, founder of Blackland Distillery, spent 15 years as an attorney before he came to the decision to enter culinary school. "It didn't take long for me to realize that I didn't want to work in a kitchen," Kypreos said. He transitioned into a sommelier certification and eventually started to study distilling, and then in 2019 he opened Blackland.

"Nothing about our distillery looks like a typical distillery. There's not a lot of copper, everything is stainless steel, and of course our automated stills," said Kypreos. The distillery itself is a modern marvel, as Blackland uses the iStill system for distillation. The iStill is an automated distillation system that gives the distillery the ability to automate cut points and proof percentage, using a digital interface that ultimately allows a distiller to easily replicate their process. "With the iStill, you get a clean, consistent product, which is what we were looking for," said Kypreos.

One of the other unique elements of Blackland is their use of triticale, a wheat-rye hybrid grain. Kypreos said, "We're barreling a 100% triticale whiskey right now and I can't wait for it to come out. I don't know anyone else in Texas that is doing that."

Their current bourbon and rye whiskeys are a blend of 80% Minnesota sourced five-year whiskeys and 20% of Blackland's younger, self-produced distillate. "The bourbon that I've sourced is very wheat heavy. It has no barley in it and the rye is a 100% malted rye. The thing that I like about the flavor profiles is that the creaminess of the wheat within our triticale distillate cuts into the spiciness of the rye. This isn't one of those 90/100% super ryes, which I like, but I also like that we're making something a little different." Kypreos also told me that the goal is to move to 100% produced distillate as soon as possible. "More than anything, I'm a big believer in transparency."

All of the ingredients for Blackland's spirits, sans the sourced whiskey portion, are entirely locally sourced. "It's probably my food background and my wine background, but ingredients are everything. For me, I wanted to focus on grains and how they were being cooked and finished. I thought I could do something really different if I approached it right. The thing I'm the most excited about is our 100% triticale that we're going to call Blackland Whiskey. It's such a different flavor and it's really exciting."

BLACKLAND RYE 100

Blend of 80% 4-year-old rye from Minnesota and 20% young rye from Blackland; their young rye consists of 80% Texas rye and 20% triticale. The 100 proof version is only available at the distillery. The same basic tasting notes will apply to the Blackland Rye, but the 100 is definitely more robust.

PROOF: 100

NOSE: Very light on the nose, vanilla buttercream icing, dried leaves, cinnamon apple baked oatmeal

PALATE: Herbal, creamy, candy-corn macaron, cinnamon-sugar bagel, new leather.

BLACKLAND BOURBON

Blend of 80% 4-year-old bourbon from Minnesota and 20% young bourbon from Blackland; their young bourbon consists of 80% Texas yellow corn and 20% triticale.

PROOF: 83

NOSE: Vanilla bean, sweet butter.

PALATE: Grilled corn on the cob, rich, the slightest of spice, lemon thyme, warm butterscotch syrup (the kind you put on ice cream and it gets all melty... damn, now I want ice cream, bourbon and ice cream).

DOUBLE BLACK COWBOY COLD BREW

Megan McClinton is a North Texas native with over fifteen years of service industry experience. Now working as General Manager of Blackland Distillery's tasting room, she is focused on education and continuing to help build the Fort Worth craft community.

"With this cocktail," she explains, "I wanted something anyone could put together at home for a quick, dark, and strong pick-me-up. The salt marries the ingredients and brings out subtle notes of spice from the rye. I love a little citrus with my black coffee, and the expressed lemon peel adds a nice aroma and a touch of acidity."

1¾ oz. Blackland Rye

¾ oz. Mr. Black Cold Brew Coffee Liqueur

1 oz. Avoca RTD Cold Brew

1 generous pinch kosher salt

1. In a rocks glass, combine all of the ingredients, add ice, and stir to combine.

2. Garnish with an expressed lemon twist.

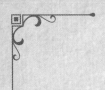

DEEP ELLUM DISTILLERY

DEEP ELLUM, TO ME, WILL ALWAYS BE WHERE all of the "kids" in Dallas grew up. Even before we could legally drink, Deep Ellum was the place that you would go to find your community. Over the past few decades, this historic hub of live music, art, and theater has evolved alongside the newly embraced culinary arts. It makes sense that the first craft brewery in Dallas opened in Deep Ellum and it certainly makes sense that the brewery begat the first craft distillery in Dallas.

John Reardon founded Deep Ellum Brewery during the height of the craft beer boom in the early 2000s. While not originally part of the plan, once he saw a batch of his beer dumped because it didn't meet their standards, he thought to himself that there must be a way to still use this beer. Enter distilling.

Genevieve the Dragon, their 1,500-gallon combination pot and column still, was named in honor of a political blogger who took exception to the slogan "Goes Down Easy" being used for Deep Ellum Brewery's Dallas Blonde Ale. While the majority of the spirit coming out of Deep Ellum has been vodka, they've also been patiently waiting for their whiskey to age. "We started out on the brewing side, but when we moved into the new space in 2016, we started to focus more on distilling," said head distiller Stuart Vance. "As brewers we loved to do the separation of the barley and we have access to a lot of fermenters, so we wanted to do an Irish-inspired whiskey." With this release, Deep Ellum Distillery is looking to add whiskey to the ongoing story of historic Deep Ellum.

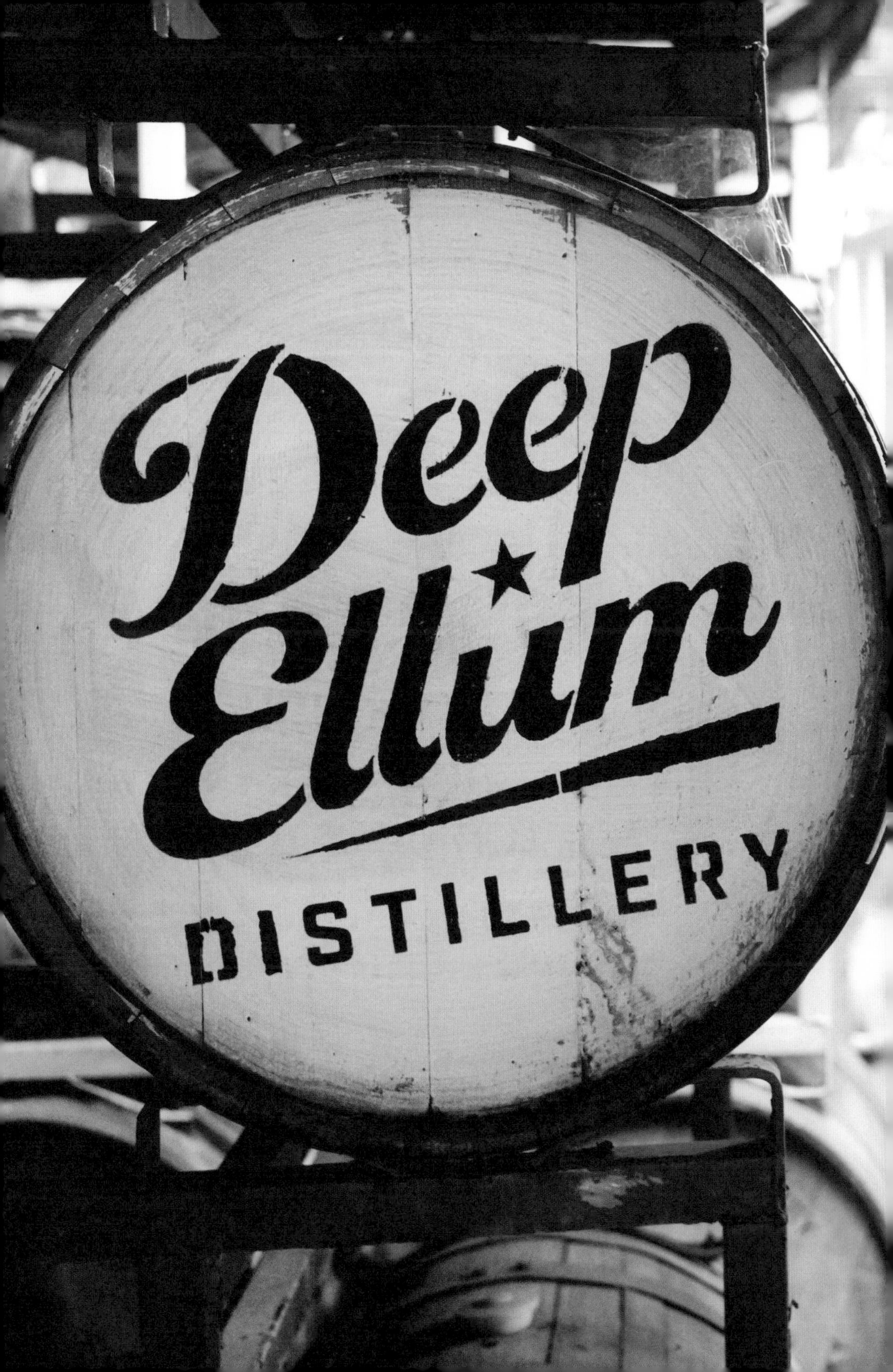
Deep
Ellum
DISTILLERY

LEADBELLY WHISKEY

The whiskey itself is made from 51% malted barley and 49% unmalted barley mash and one of the only Irish-inspired whiskeys in the state. This is named after Huddie "Lead Belly" Ledbetter, a legendary blues musician who used to frequent Deep Ellum around the time he was imprisoned for murder in 1918. But don't worry, according to tradition, he won his early release in 1925 by singing a song for the governor of Texas. This is entirely grain to glass and only uses Texas products for their double-distilled, pot still-style whiskey.

 PROOF: 94

 NOSE: Sweet, barnyard hay, musty cellar, sourdough, baking spice.

 PALATE: Sawdust, dried tea leaves, light toasted oak, medicinal, lemon drop candy finish.

LEAD ★ BELLY

WHISKEY

DEEP ELLUM SPIRITS

LIMITED RELEASE

10/89   20/20

SINGLE BARREL

TEXAS

SMALL
BATCH   **WHISKEY**   HAND
BOTTLED

DISTILLED IN IRISH TRADITION USING MALTED &
UNMALTED BARLEY AND AGED IN BOURBON BARRELS
FOR AN EXTRA SMOOTH FINISH

PROOF ●   ALC. BY VOL. ● 750 ML

OLD FASHIONED 6/11/20

FIRESTONE & ROBERTSON

ORIGIN STORIES ARE VITAL when it comes to the description of a company or a person. But are they what truly matter? One of my favorite musical artists is the Beastie Boys. Their origin story is a complicated one and they'll be the first ones to tell you about how they were the "white guys" who were picked to increase the popularity of the rap genre as a whole, about how they made some terrible choices and regretted their actions in the beginning, and about how sickeningly immature they were. They began as shitty little misogynists, and then they grew. They grew as artists, but more importantly, they grew as people. "I'd rather be a hypocrite than never have changed," Ad Rock once said.

Firestone & Robertson was featured in my last book, *Texas Cocktails*. They had just opened their incredible Whiskey Ranch and they had established themselves as a force to be reckoned with in the whiskey world. When they first began, they decided that they were going to go after the most popular whiskey in Texas, Crown Royal, and they were going to do everything they could to take back some of that established brand's market share. They wanted more Texans drinking whiskey from a Texas company and drinking less Canadian whisky. Did you know that, for a very long time, Crown Royal sold more product in Texas than in Canada? Yeah, me either.

Leonard Firestone and Troy Robertson became friends because their kids were in the same playgroup, and one day they independently made plans to visit the same distillery. According to their website, "Troy got there first, and while chatting with the owner, discovered that 'another Fort Worth guy' had scheduled a visit the following week. Imagine Troy's surprise when he found out it was Leonard. 'I hear you want to get into the whiskey business?' Troy said when he called Leonard later. Leonard, who'd told no one but his wife about his plans, was floored. We got together for lunch the next day and quickly discovered we had the same vision for creating truly Texas whiskeys, and the same obsession with old-fashioned craftsmanship."

When Firestone & Robertson started, they were working out their mash bill and working toward distilling their own whiskey, but they also found themselves with the opportunity to source a product they believed could be blended into something good enough to replace Crown as the most popular brand in Texas, and so they launched the first distillery in North Texas.

Since then, Firestone & Robertson has moved the majority of their operations to the friendly confines of Glen Garden Country Club, taking over the entire course and dubbing it Whiskey Ranch. This might be the most beautiful distillery I've ever been to. You drive up to the tasting room, passing a pristine golf course, and you arrive at the top of this random hill. I say random because we don't really do "hills" in North Texas, but there you are, next to an awe-inspiring distillery, a gorgeous ranch-style building holding the tasting room and bar and then you see a crystal clear, unobstructed view of Downtown Fort Worth. It's magical.

When I first stepped on the property three years ago, my first thought was *Man, this is going to be a huge deal for the Texas whiskey tourism industry*. I've been to some of the time-honored distilleries in Kentucky and Tennessee, and this is one of the few places in Texas that makes you feel like you do when you're on the Kentucky Bourbon Trail.

As you walk through the grounds of Whiskey Ranch, it feels like hallowed ground. You can almost tell that Ben Hogan and Bryon Nelson learned how to play golf here. The main artery of Whiskey Ranch is The Courtyard, and it was designed to maintain an unobstructed view of Downtown Fort Worth. They've leaned into this as well. Before COVID-19 hit, they were hosting live music, opening up the whole ranch on the weekends, and they had just built a beautiful outdoor kitchen and were hosting cocktail and barbecue classes with Matt Pittman,

the Meat Church bro. If you fancy yourself a Texas whiskey vacation, I couldn't recommend Whiskey Ranch any higher. It's truly special and you know that the second you arrive.

TX Whiskey is... challenging to talk about. TX Whiskey isn't. Firestone and Robertson would tell you the same thing. They backed their way into creating a product that is not made in Texas (although the plan is to make all of their own everything sooner than later) but is ultimately viewed as Texas whiskey. Why wouldn't it be? It literally says it on the bottle. This is why they're a very interesting part of the Texas whiskey story. They were one of the first brands in Texas to achieve big-time distribution, which was an incredible achievement and benefitted the Texas whiskey industry more than I can state. In a time when there were not a lot of people who realized that we made whiskey in Texas, TX became an incredible billboard for the industry as a whole. They were in liquor stores and restaurants all over and their bottle was screaming "We make whiskey in Texas! Hey! Look! Texas. Whiskey. TX Whiskey. We make whiskey in Texas!" Couple that with some very impressive awards being claimed by a variety of Texas distillers, they helped to truly announce the presence of Texas whiskey. Just with the bottle. The bottle that, while perfectly marketed, was also the cause of a whole lot of hubbub.

"I was in grad school, working on a PhD in chemistry at UT Southwestern. I'm from Louisville and I'm third generation in the industry. I started making beer and whiskey at home and kinda got enamored by it all. I decided to leave school with my Master's early and I decided to join Troy and Leonard," Rob Arnold, Firestone & Robertson's master distiller told me. He was actually looking for his own place to open his own small distillery. He was talking to a developer when he was told about Firestone and Robertson's plans. He found Firestone's email online and emailed him asking for advice on raising money in exchange for his advice on making whiskey. They weren't whiskey makers, and they needed a distiller. The path had revealed itself.

Arnold came on board and helped build the distillery, Dave Pickerell was hired to consult for a bit, and they started making whiskey in February 2012. Arnold quickly became their cheat code and one of the first things that he did was tackle the yeast portion of the distillate. He worked with Texas Christian University's biology department to isolate about 100 different yeasts and, using DNA sequencing, narrowed the options down to five. In a series of blind taste tests, Firestone, Robertson, and Arnold all picked the same strain, a yeast they found on a pecan. How Texan is that? "I know it sounds like marketing crap, but that's just what happened," Arnold said.

Arnold says he'll always consider himself a whiskey maker. Well, that, and a scientist. "There's a big difference between a distiller and a whiskey maker and I'm definitely a whiskey maker, but truly, I'll always be more of a scientist." He went back to school to get his PhD, but this time at Texas A&M and this time in plant breeding and genetics.

"We're currently trying to breed specific varieties for whiskey. The breeders of traditional yellow dent corn never once thought about whiskey distillers and heirloom corn, and the use of heirloom corn in whiskey is all about flavor, but the problem is that the yields are typically quite small. We're trying to merge these two things. For years we've been going through the process of screening some novel hybrids, created by the labs at Texas A&M, that have a lot of genetics that are closely related to the heirlooms found in Central and South America. We've narrowed it down to three varieties that are in the process of trial at our farm down in Hillsboro. By 2022, all of the corn we use will be these proprietary novel hybrids. So no more commercial corn for TX Whiskey. We're also reviving an old Texas heirloom called Hillsboro Blue and White that hasn't been grown in Texas in decades.

"My ultimate goal is to find ways to bring heirloom flavors into higher yielding varieties so that we're making corn that's specifically for making whiskey. It's not just corn, it's also wheat and barley and other grains, but we're starting with corn. Modern varieties of corn don't make bad whiskies by any means, but it's a very diluted form of the corn we could be working with," explained Arnold.

I asked if this work and these varietals were going to be readily available for people who don't work for Firestone & Robertson. "We're actually going to create a breeding program here. We have 100 acres of land so we're going to start growing and trying to breed varieties here. I don't want this to be just for TX, I want this to be more widely available and I want to prove that research is valuable." Arnold told me that over the past couple of years, he's been able to dedicate the majority of his time to research. They're also running oak seasoning trials on their property, experimenting with various char levels, and trialing different barrel types.

"For some of these massive changes to actually take place, we're going to have to have an impact in Kentucky and in Tennessee. It's just harkening back to the way it used to be. It was all heirlooms before 1920. We got out of Prohibition

and about ten years later corn production went from heirlooms to hybrids, the beginning of industrial techniques, and the use of synthetic fertilizers and this ridiculous output of corn when America started producing for yield. We lost a lot in terms of the quality of raw ingredients," Arnold said.

In August 2019, Pernod Ricard USA announced that they had acquired Firestone & Robertson Distilling Company. This was one of the biggest acquisitions in the history of the Texas whiskey industry. "When this was run by Troy and Leonard the blend just sold like crazy," said Arnold. "They definitely saw what was happening. What they created became this brand that became massive. I don't blame them, I agree with them, but we were no longer focused on that. Pernod has been the opposite. We've spent thousands of dollars on innovation with them. The company has changed a lot."

The infamous TX Whiskey blend is an absolute lightning rod in the Texas whiskey industry. There have been countless take downs of the spirit and it's been a heated topic of discussion since the day it launched. "I hate to harp on this, and we don't lie, but I'll admit that, for the uninformed consumer, it's hard to see that our blend is not distilled in Texas. We're moving to a system that will make it 100% distilled in Texas. When Pernod came in, they're the ones who said immediately that we needed to address some things about the process. They liked the product, but they said there were some problems with the perception and they wanted us to fix it so that we all could stand behind the product," Arnold told me. "When we launched, it was so new that this wasn't even a topic of discussion. We never put Texas Blended Whiskey on the label on purpose, but we also didn't realize the snowball effect. The industry has changed so much and we definitely want to be a part of the transparency and authenticity movement.

"When I realized what was going on, it didn't sit right and I've always wanted to address it. It was so nice that one of the mandates from Pernod Richard to buy the company was that we literally needed to address it. We knew that we owed it to the category to make things right."

One of the most interesting concepts coming out of TX Whiskey, fittingly, is their Experimental Series. The plan is to do themed releases, all based on exploring a specific element: organic versus biodynamic versus conventional agriculture; the difference between five years in the barrel versus four years in the barrel versus three years; muscatel versus toasted oak versus sherry finishes. There's a new focus on experimentation, research, and distilling down whiskey to its core

ingredients to focus on finding ways to enhance them. "We're discussing all sorts of options. I don't even know if we're just going to be a bourbon and rye whiskey distillery, if we're going to make a lot more than that, maybe even things that are not whiskey."

The biggest difference between the Firestone & Robertson I first visited years ago and this one is freedom. The opportunities here are endless. They have the resources and, for now, they have the trust of those resources. Firestone & Robertson is currently working on some of the coolest experiments in all of whiskey, let alone Texas.

I'll let Rob Arnold have the final word: "We want to make our mark as Texas whiskey, but more so, we want to help push this category forward. I think we have an opportunity here to be known as a whiskey region. We're all taking very different approaches, but as long as we're all being transparent and honest and pushing the category, it's going to be amazing. Spirits evolve. We just want to help continue the evolution of the spirit."

TX BOURBON
STRAIGHT BOURBON

The flagship bourbon is 100% grain to glass, made with corn, red wheat, and six-row malt, aged somewhere around 4 to 5 years.

PROOF: 90

NOSE: The water you cook corn in, soft caramel candies, applesauce, grilled peaches.

PALATE: The sweet and gooey part of pecan pie, toasted oak, silky, brown butter, dusty.

TX BOURBON
STRAIGHT BOURBON
BARREL PROOF

Straight from the barrel, uncut and unfiltered, each batch will be slightly different; these notes are for batch one.

PROOF: 127.4

NOSE: Grilled corn, fresh-cut Granny Smith apples, cinnamon-brown sugar bars.

PALATE: Black licorice, heavy oak, apple baklava, mouth-coating, mince pie, long finish.

TX BOURBON PX
SHERRY FINISHED

TX Straight Bourbon aged 4 years and finished for an additional 8 months in Pedro Ximénez sherry casks.

PROOF: 101.6

NOSE: Stewed raisins, dry plum, Almond Joy, cinnamon-baked apples, pipe tobacco.

PALATE: Mild toasted oak, toffee, tupelo honey, dark chocolate-covered apricot, No. 3 dark maple syrup

TX EXPERIMENTAL SERIES– STRAIGHT RYE

The first expression in the TX Experimental Series, this is uncut and unfiltered 100% rye based, with 85% rye and 15% malted rye; only available at the distillery in 375ml bottles.

PROOF: 126.1

NOSE: Fresh plum, ceylon cinnamon bark, clove, peach-infused hibiscus tea, roasted almonds.

PALATE: Old cigar box, ground cardamom, hint of chocolate covered sea salt caramel.

THOROUGHBRED

Kevin Gray, the creator of Cocktail Enthusiast and the Beverage Director at The Hitchcock in Dallas, devised The Thoroughbred as a Texas-y take on the classic Saratoga and a very easy way to make a delicious drink in equal parts. Sub a rye for a spicier approach.

1 oz. TX Bourbon

1 oz. Cognac

1 oz. sweet vermouth

2 dashes aromatic bitters

1. Combine all of the ingredients in a mixing glass with ice, stir, and strain into a coupe.

2. Garnish with an orange peel.

TEXAS WHISKEY & AGRICULTURAL SUSTAINABILITY

DR. ROB ARNOLD

The current agricultural system is broken.

Corn, wheat, and rice account for 50% of the world's consumption of calories and protein, and 95% of the world's food needs are provided by just 30 plant species. The genetic diversity of these crops that nurture us is extremely low compared to what is actually available in nature. This exaggerated use of a few, genetically closed crop varieties is not an artifact of man's tactful dominance over nature. Rather, it is the result of our desire to simplify and restrict nature, with the hope that we can increase yields while simultaneously reducing our workload. On the surface, this desire has succeeded; in recent decades we have seen agricultural yields increase to previously unimaginable levels. But there is no such thing as a free lunch. Nature will eventually fight back. Natural selection ensures that populations characterized by both widespread presence and low genetic diversity will not persevere. Nature ensures and fosters balance, not dominance.

If our agricultural system does not acknowledge this and make concerted efforts to balance our needs with those of nature, then we will pay a costly price. Decimating disease, nutritional deficiency, environmental collapse; such outcomes await crops and people alike if the current system prevails. But there is hope, and it lies with *orphans*. Those forgotten plants that were both progenitors for and examples of important food sources to the thousands of generations before us. They are an important means for achieving a resilient, sustainable, nutritious, and flavorful agriculture. We have forgotten them, but nature has not. Nature remembers what such genetic diversity can bring to an ecosystem, and to the people who cultivate them for sustenance. It's time for our agricultural system to work with nature—even foster it—not against it.

I'll provide one example here—the pursuit for perennial grain crops. We can greatly reduce soil degradation and erosion by converting our staple grain crops—such as corn, wheat, and rice—from annual to perennial varieties. Currently, though, the overwhelming majority of farmland is planted with annuals. On the surface, this seems practical. In the span of one year or less, annual crops are planted from seed, they grow until fruit or seed is produced, and then they die. Before or after their demise, we harvest that fruit or seed as food. Annuals have a major advantage, which is as true today as it was at the dawn of agriculture. Namely, because seed is planted every year, that allowed farmers to select the best seeds from each harvest for sowing the following year. This artificial selection meant that farmers could improve their crops—and therefore their yields—from season to season. But the need to replant every year comes with cost, the most impactful of which is on the soil. For millennia, hoes and plows have been used to clear the farmland of any vegetation before sowing. The result is a devastating disruption to the balance and ecosystem of the soil, leading to carbon loss (ending up in the atmosphere as CO_2), erosion, poor fertility, and fertilizer/pesticide runoff.

One solution to soil erosion and degradation is perennial crops. Such plants do not have to be sown each year, and therefore do not require the annual hoeing or plowing of the land. Perennials become established, growing long and integrated roots that actually protect the soil from erosion and degradation. The challenge, though, is how can we convert our most staple annual crops into perennials? To start, we can turn to orphans. Specifically, we turn to the wild, progenitor species of our modern-day varieties. These forebears are indeed perennials and hidden within their genes are the tools needed for converting our staple annual crops. Perennial wheat is currently being developed at the Land Institute in Kansas. Renowned barley breeder Dr. Pat Hayes at Oregon State University has considered how perennial barley might be created. And here in Texas, Dr. Seth Murray (my PhD advisor) at Texas A&M is developing perennial corn.

The resources that orphan crops provide for developing perennial versions of our staple crops is just one example of how they can lead to a more sustainable agriculture. There are many others. Heirloom and wild versions of our modern varieties might also provide the genetic machinery for pest, heat, and drought resistance. Such traits can lead to less chemical use on the farm, and they serve as Darwinian ammunition to battle the effects of climate change.

But this is an essay within a book about whiskey. So, what does all of this have to do with whiskey? After all, the whiskey industry uses a relatively small amount of grain compared to others, such as animal feed and fuel ethanol. What exactly can our industry do to meaningfully support sustainable agriculture, which I argue can be fueled by the genetic resources within the biodiversity of orphans?

Where whiskey is uniquely positioned is that it, along with beer, is arguably the most romanticized and consumer-facing product made from grain. While the whiskey industry just barely moves the needle on global grain sales, it does pull at the heartstrings in a way that could potentially inspire change that echoes far beyond our copper-hued confines. Sustainable agriculture needs a new face; a passionate one that people can identify with, so that they will continue to embrace the movement and work against the current industrial model. Orphan crops can both serve as this face while simultaneously providing the biological tools needed to achieve sustainability. And the whiskey industry can serve as a powerful medium for communicating and supporting the story and importance of their genetic biodiversity.

The whiskey industry is built on four grain types, all of which are dominant players in the global commodity feed, food, fuel, and malt markets: corn, wheat, rye, and barley. In no way am I suggesting that we get rid of these crops. On the contrary, what I'm suggesting is that we can use the biodiversity that still exists within these species, as well as their close relatives, to generate more sustainable, and more flavorful, versions of them. The introduction of perennial corn, wheat, rye, and barley will take many decades of research, but in theory it's possible. Introgression of traits from heirloom and wild varieties into modern, high yielding ones is already a proven method. Still, both pursuits garner little attention from the global scientific community. Part of this is due to the inherent technical challenges. But another reason is that commercial breeding companies do not invest in such pursuits. In general, only public breeding programs do. But even there, it is a constant challenge to secure funds for such high-risk, long-term research.

Here is where Texas distillers specifically can play a pivotal role in this story. We have some of the top agricultural and plant breeding scientists in the world at our state's land-grant university—Texas A&M. (The "A" in A&M does stand for *agricultural*, after all.)

The Texas whiskey industry could play a major role in supporting the work of these scientists. Could this be financial? Of course. TX Whiskey financially supported my PhD dissertation in plant breeding, as well as our head blender Ale Ochoa's MS thesis, both of which were completed at Texas A&M. But you don't need a student to support their work. Texas A&M releases varieties of corn, wheat, milo, and rice. Working with a grower to source and grow their varieties for our Texas whiskeys (whether they are varieties from Texas A&M directly, or are commercial hybrids produced from Texas A&M inbred lines) is an important role we can play to support their endeavors. And we can also support their long-term initiatives. Perennial corn would of course qualify. So would a concerted effort to support the breeding and selection of new barley and rye that are adapted to the Texas environment.

Beyond financial support, we can and should act as communicators and champions of their research goals. We have a certain platform as Texas whiskey distillers, and when we talk, there is a good chance *some* people (especially Texans) will listen. Let's spread the message and goals of our state's public agricultural and plant breeding scientists. Our craft starts with a grain crop, and it's our responsibility to support those who ensure its legacy and sustainability.

Lastly, as innovative Texas distillers, we should look at orphan crops not just as a source of genetic diversity for breeding, but as a source for mashing, fermentation, distillation, and maturation. Whiskey produced from quinoa—an orphan crop—already exists. Further, whiskey could be distilled from lesser-known orphans, such as millet, tef, or the perennial wheatgrass created by the Land Institute called Kernza (which is already being used to make beer). We can and should do more as an industry to promote and support such unknown whiskey styles, and the sustainable endeavors they support.

Sustainable agriculture needs a new face; a passionate one that people can identify with, so that they will embrace the movement and work against the current industrial model. Orphan crops can both serve as this face while simultaneously providing the biological tools needed to achieve sustainability. But someone needs to share and support their story. Texas whiskey distillers are in a rare position to do just this.

Dr. Rob Arnold is the Master Distiller at the Firestone & Robertson Distillery and is the author of The Terroir of Whiskey: A Distiller's Journey into the Flavor of Place.

GRAYSON

FULL DISCLOSURE: I'M A PART OWNER OF GRAYSON. I found myself discussing Texas whiskey with Brandon Davis and former Yankee great, Arlington Bowie's own, Vernon Wells. "We were already in the wine business so we were entertaining the idea of making brandy with some of our grapes. We met with a few distilleries in Northern California and it just wound up not being a good financial decision. Fast forward to the following year and Vernon says 'I really love this Texas whiskey. What if we bought some barrels and did a Texas whiskey?'" Davis told me.

Here's where I came in. A friend of a friend introduced me to Davis and explained the story to me. Davis and I met up for lunch and started hatching a plan for what would become Grayson. We all live in Texas, Wells and I are native and Davis got here as quickly as he could and we wanted to honor this great state and the makers here. We had an opportunity to pay homage to this industry we all love and we wanted to highlight multiple distillers at once. Grayson is the first Texas Blended Bourbon.

The first thing I did was call Ironroot (see page 113) because, personally, I think they are the best bourbon blenders in the state. We headed up to Denison and we told Robert and Jonathan Likerish, founders of Ironroot, what we were hoping to do and asked if they would be interested in partnering. We must have been charming enough, because they said yes. "As soon as we started talking to them and tasting through some barrels, we knew it was the perfect fit," Davis said.

Ultimately, we chose a blend that has Ironroot's Harbinger, Balcones, Pot Still Bourbon, and Lone Elm's Single Barrel Wheat Whiskey, and it's damn good if I do say so myself. We wanted to be a part of this incredible industry, but we also knew that there are people who are far better at making whiskey than we ever will be, so why not work with and highlight what they do? This is our way of showing the world what an amalgamation of the best whiskeys in Texas can be. We're awfully proud of the spirits coming out of this state and are thrilled to be a part of this story.

At Grayson, we do our best to continuously put out incredible blends of Texas whiskeys. Maybe this is why I'm a little partial to the concept of blending houses and private labels. The next edition of Grayson may be the same whiskey, or it may be a different blend. It will always, however, be a primarily Texas whiskey. Our whiskey is cask strength because how the hell would we pay our respects to Texas with something under 119 proof? Damn right.

GRAYSON

A 100% Texas wheat-heavy, blended bourbon, with Ironroot
Republic Harbinger, Balcones Pot Still, and Lone Elm Single
Barrel Wheat Whiskey.

PROOF: 119.4

NOSE: Raisins, barrel-aged maple syrup, beignet-flavored coffee
grounds, subtle hint of the inside of new cowboy boots, jalapeño
jelly.

PALATE: Super sweet initially with syrupy waffle notes, moves into
a spiced cider with allspice, cloves, cinnamon, and nutmeg, brown
butter into an almost burnt pecan, sweet wheat and fennel finish.

HERMAN MARSHALL

HERMAN BECKLEY AND MARSHALL LOUIS discovered their mutual interest in whiskey at a Starbucks, where they were part of a group of friends who got together there on weekends. Beckley was in the computer industry and Louis, who hails from South Africa, comes from a family of winemakers. "We illegally began in Herman's garage. But, I don't know many whiskey makers who started legally," Louis recalled with laugh.

Herman Marshall is Dallas' first legal distillery since Prohibition. They started producing their first batches in 2012. "First and foremost, this was a passion project," said Russel Louis, CEO of Herman Marshall Whiskey. "We have products that have aged for four years, we have stuff in the back that's been aged for eight years. We might not have much of it, but we've been at this for a while. We also love our collaborations with our friends who own breweries."

"It's been a challenging business, competing against massive companies who've been around since Prohibition and have multimillion dollar marketing budgets. We're all small guys, but it feels like we're all part of these whiskey makers who are writing the beginnings of the history in this state. We have some incredible whiskey here and we're so proud of being one of the first ones in this industry," said Russel. When I asked about the mash bill on their bourbon, he told me it was 77% corn and 23% malted barley. "It broke down to the number of bags of each that we had at the beginning," Russel said. "There's an old handbook called *The Practical Distiller* that suggested that ratio makes for good whiskey. So we tried, we liked it, we threw some rapid age on it as much as we could and liked what came out." Also interesting to note is the use of open-air fermentation tanks that were handmade out of swamp cypress. Is "gator" an appropriate tasting note? Asking for me.

The coolest innovations here are done through collaboration. There are a handful of distilleries in Texas that are either working with breweries or are brewers themselves who moved into distilling as a line extension, but Herman Marshall was the first to work with an outside brewery. They started with a Temptress from Lakewood and the Divine Reserve from Saint Arnold shortly followed. This is a category that Texas seems to nail. I mean, I'm not a craft beer guy, but I'll put our craft beer scene up with anyone as well. It's very cool to see these crossovers and to know about future ones coming down the pike. Herman Marshall, above all else, is straightforward Texas whiskey. They're one of the original whiskey distilleries in the state and they still represent.

Herman Marshall's Texas Bourbon Whiskey won third place in the 2015 International Whisky Competition's Best Small Batch Bourbon category. They were crushing awards before most of these other whiskeys were a glimmer in a distiller's eye.

TEXAS BOURBON

The flagship whiskey of the Herman Marshall Experience; 100% grain to glass: 77% corn, 23% malted barley.

PROOF: 92

NOSE: Caramel syrup on top of vanilla bean ice cream, almond croissants, lemon meringue.

PALATE: Cafe mocha, churros, malt extract, spiced fruitcake, hint of sprouts.

HERMAN ★ MARSHALL
HAND CRAFTED SMALL BATCH WHISKEY
HM
750 ML ★ 46% ALC/VOL ★ 92 PROOF
TEXAS BOURBON WHISKEY

TEXAS RYE

Aged for at least four years in charred, new 53-gallon American white oak barrels and then bottled at 92 proof; the mash bill is 77% rye and 23% malted barley.

PROOF: 92

NOSE: Clover, vanilla cream puff, light and floral, homemade lemon icing, fabric softener.

PALATE: Light caramel, Cinnamon Toast Crunch, fresh green beans, vanilla cream eclair filling.

HM80

Designed to be their lower proof "entry" whiskey, the HM80 is 100% Texas grain to glass and is a port finished blend; mellow and approachable.

PROOF: 80

NOSE: Toasted oak, white pepper, light nose, creamed clover honey, walking by a honeysuckle bush in the spring.

PALATE: Maraschino cherries, Fig Newtons, Raisin Bran, prunes, cinnamon-stewed pears, sage, super light, green tomatoes.

TEXAS NAVEL

Herman Marshall Bourbon offers a delicious spice-forward profile to give complexity to cocktails. Trey Roland created this crowd pleaser that doesn't require you to be an avid whiskey drinker to enjoy.

2 oz. Herman Marshall Bourbon

¾ oz. light brown sugar syrup
(1:1 ratio)

¼ oz. fresh lemon juice

1 bar spoon Cointreau

2 orange peels

1. Combine all of the ingredients, except orange peels, in a cocktail shaker. Bend orange peels over the shaker to express oil and then add the expressed peels to the shaker, along with ice.

2. Shake vigorously, strain into a rocks glass over pellet ice, and garnish with an orange wheel.

IRONROOT REPUBLIC DISTILLING

THERE'S NOTHING QUITE LIKE a traditional Christmas dinner. China is on the table for its one-night-only, exclusive appearance. All sorts of bottles of all sorts of elixirs are open and being poured into only the fanciest glassware. You're doing everything you can to create new memories and soak up the essence of your family. Christmas dinner is the most magical time of the year, so, of course, that's where Robert Likarish decided to make an announcement that would forever change his life, and his family's.

"Of course he did it then. We were all at maximum happiness," said Marcia Likarish. "We were all at the table and everybody was so excited because Jonathan had just had his baby girl and had just taken an internship in Texas to start his career. Robert was about to graduate from law school and it felt like everything was moving in a very specific direction." Apparently Robert thought that the status quo would have been just a little too easy. Over that dinner he told his family that he wanted to make whiskey, and not be a lawyer. Next thing you know, they started planning a trip to Denver to visit a handful of distilleries.

Robert and Marica decided to spend Robert's final spring break in Kentucky, traipsing around the Bourbon Trail. Initially, Robert was leaning toward brandy, so they visited Huber's Starlight Distillery, located on Huber's orchard and vineyard. They had a chance to talk to the head distiller and winemaker, Ted Huber, who also happened to be a board member of the American Craft Distillers Association. He said that if they were going to be serious about starting a distillery, they should visit the small guys, not the bigger distilleries. They started to plot out their trip, including a handful of smaller operations, but most importantly, it included a stop at Vendome.

Vendome Copper & Brass Works is the premiere maker of stills in the United States and one of the best on the planet. "We told them we were interested in opening a distillery and they wanted to know what kind steel we wanted and what kind of capacity we were thinking and we just stood there like a deer in headlights. When we walked out, we literally had no idea what had just happened, but he put us on the list," said Robert. "He told us it would be at least two years before we could have a still made, so when we left, we didn't really even think about it again."

In the midst of this, Jonathan, the engineer of the family, had started gathering all of the books he could find on distilling, fermentation, and brewing sciences. He then turned to his brother and said, "Alright, chief, if you're serious about this, you're going to have to get down to Texas so we can visit the... let me check my notes... two distilleries in Texas making whiskey." (I'm paraphrasing.)

Marcia was able to get a hold of Chip Tate and set up a private tour for Robert at Balcones. By the end of the meeting, Tate had talked Robert into hiring him as a consultant. "They had only been in business for about nine months and I'm pretty sure they didn't even have any whiskey out. But he certainly had some interesting ideas on barrels and how to approach aging in Texas. Early on, he was very instrumental in guiding us in certain directions," Robert said. One of the very first topics they needed to tackle was determining exactly what they would be distilling with.

Initially, both Ironroot and Balcones were going to buy Forsyth pot stills and split the shipping. But all of a sudden Edrington showed up and placed a huge order with Forsyth and the wait time went from one year to four or more. Tate turned to the Likarish family and said, "Nah, y'all... I've got this. I'll build the still my damn self." (Still paraphrasing.) But unfortunately Tate's confidence that he could manifest a pot still out of thin air did not extend to the Likarishs' loan officer. The bank said they wouldn't fund them unless they had a "known" company building their still. So Marcia called Vendome, fully prepared to plead their case with their tail firmly between their legs. "We were next on the list," she said.

Vendome was about to order the pieces to build their still and was literally emailing the Likarishs the following week to nail down specifics. They told Marcia that if they could finalize the capacity and the shape of their still, they'd have it to them within four months. Fun fact: at the time, Vendome had a three-year waiting list for any new orders. Game on.

During all of this, since Robert had no real idea when they'd actually be starting their distillery, he started grad school at Austin College in Sherman. While he was in the area, Robert was introduced to the wine history in the Denison area, just up the road from the school. "The first spirits I really got into were Cognac and Armagnac because when my dad would go to wine tastings with my mom, the guy would take him into the back to go drink brandy. My dad would give us bottles for Christmas and so I always had a taste for brandy," Robert said.

During his spiritual (get it?) exploration, he had taken a brandy class from tenth-generation Cognac maker, Hubert Germain-Robin, the co-founder of the Germain-Robin brandy house and Nancy "The Nose" Fraley.

So as the still was being made, they started looking for a place to build their distillery. Since Robert liked what he had heard about the history, they visited a few vineyards in the Denison area and learned that in the late 1800s a resident of Denison, T.V. Munson, had literally saved the French wine industry from a devastating disease called phylloxera. Munson had developed rootstocks, which allowed the French to continue to grow their ancient varietals. Munson used specific, native Texas grapes because the soils closely matched the limestone soils in French vineyards and the native Texan grapes were highly tolerant of both higher levels of pH and were phylloxera-resistant. In 1888, Munson was named a *Chevalier du Mérite Agricole* of the French Legion of Honor, an order of merit bestowed by the French Republic for outstanding contributions to agriculture and Cognac, France, became the sister city to Denison, all because of Munson's "iron root."

With this story as inspiration, and knowing that they wanted to make some brandy at some point, they decided that Denison would be the home of Ironroot Republic Distilling. After consulting with Fraley, Robert and Jonathan decided to start working on a plan to make Texas whiskey. While hearing more established distillers talking about grabbing 5-gallon barrels and throwing them into Texas rickhouses to mitigate oak extraction and wood impact, they realized the French distilling methods were essentially the opposite approach. "When we started seeing what the French were doing, it started clicking," Robert told me. Instead of amplifying the aging process, they chose to slow it down.

Jonathan said, "One of the big misconceptions about Texas whiskey is that people say because the angel share in Texas is double than this place or that place, it ages twice as fast. In some aspects, sure, but certainly not in all aspects. It's kind of somewhere in between, and there is a mountain of other factors, so our use of French techniques, like elévage, was us trying to learn the difference between extraction and actual maturation."

Part of the French technique is to mix entire vintages together. Then, they'll proof it down by 1% and put it back in the barrel. As it gets older they'll move it to older barrels, to start to lessen the oak extraction, and, generally, those barrels will start going up in size—we're talking 200-gallon barrels and larger. Once they're in the largest barrels, they'll start proofing in cask. The goal is to drop the proof somewhere around 1% or 2% a year.

When Ironroot started, 53-gallon new white American oak barrels were all but impossible to find. Fraley made a call to Independent Stave, but at the time, only preexisting clients could buy barrels from Independent Stave. Independent Stave did, however, agree to work with Ironroot, with this one teeny, itsy bitsy caveat—they had to agree to purchase more European oak barrels than American oak barrels. On the downside, these barrels were twice as expensive, but, on the plus side, the European oak was yard aged for over four years. They initially bought eighty barrels and only fifteen of them were American oak, but it got them in the system and they hoped that their next order could be closer to 50/50. Oh! And they were also forced to buy their new American oak barrels with high-end toast profiles. Fun, huh?

Now that the barrels were sorted, they needed to figure out how to tackle the distillate portion of the process. Ironroot's cheat code became their use of heirloom corn. When they started trying to figure out their mash bill, they decided they would get the best effect by utilizing Fraley's blending theories. She loved the idea of multiple mash bills from a blending standpoint, and she started working Robert and Jonathan through a classic blending triangle that one would use in whiskey, perfume, and coffee.

"I had read an article about moonshiners in the Appalachians and how they were using this special type of corn called Bloody Butcher and it seemed like with heirloom corn we were just scratching the surface," Jonathan said. Marcia began to research heirloom corn and find sources to procure it. Ironroot was truly making a brand of whiskey unseen in Texas, utilizing methods that no one else was using.

All of the Ironroot batches are individually created. "It's more like painting than anything else," Jonathan said. "Like if you're trying to make a certain color, and, traditionally, you just use these two colors to make it, but you could also try to come at it from a different angle. Each of the profiles is going to be consistent, but there are slight variables within each batch. When you are trying to blend to

a bell curve, the greater the number of barrels, the less the outliers are going to impact it. But we're a small distillery, so a 20-barrel blend will have more variance than a 1,000-barrel blend." It's more like cooking by feel then by following a recipe. Then again, I know damn well I'd rather have a burger that Thomas Keller made than one of his recipes that I tried to follow.

The technique started to pick up some steam around the state. The distillers in Texas incorporating elévage are creating something quite special. The basis of this technique is the idea that any water that is added to the distillate during aging needs to add something to the flavor profile of the whiskey. The water needs to be incorporated in a way that its role is more than simply taking proof away. There's a strong bite to a lot of Texas whiskeys and this technique is one of the most consistent in its ability to mellow out that obnoxious punch that has long given Texas whiskey a bad name. Also, in the process of proofing within their barrels, they are individually touching and monitoring their barrels far more often than other makers in the state. They are incredibly engaged in their whiskey from the beginning.

The distillery finally opened in 2014 when they bought an old boat dealership right off the highway. It's far, far more charming than it sounds. That same year Marcia—aka the Mother of Texas Whiskey—officially joined the team. At Ironroot, the Likarishs mash, ferment, distill, barrel-age, and bottle on site. Everything they make is from high-quality heirloom and non-GMO corn from local farms. Soon, Ironroot will be moving into their new location, a 20,000-square-foot building in the heart of downtown Denison. This will be one of the most impressive distilleries in Texas and will serve as a cornerstone for their community for years to come.

Ironroot has won countless awards including World's Best Corn Whisky in 2017 and 2019, 2019 and 2020 Craft Whiskey Distillery of the year from *USA Today*, and Jonathan was also a finalist for Master Distiller/Master Blender of the year. Then Ironroot Republic Distilling Harbinger Straight Bourbon was named World's Best Bourbon at the World Whiskies Awards in February 2020. It changed everything.

The World Whiskies Awards are one of the most highly regarded competitions in the world and are judged by a panel of leading journalists and industry experts. "We sold out of everything we could bottle," Robert told me. They won this award less than a month before shelter in place orders were being enacted across the state and before the full brunt of COVID-19 hit the craft distilling industry. While I'm sure they would have loved to have been able to take their victory lap, it sure made it easier to stay in business as others around them struggled. It was the best of times, it was the worst of times.

Ironroot is my go-to. If I'm ever on a mission to change someone's mind about Texas whiskey, it's Ironroot. If you're going to tell me that "Texas whiskey is too hot," I'm going to give you Ironroot. Then you'll love it and only then will I grab the bottle and say "That was 122 proof, sucker!" Ironroot's best bourbon award was a culmination of thousands of hours of hard work and dedication to create a style of whiskey that can only exist in Texas, and it didn't surprise me in the least. If you have any preconceived notions about the bourbon coming out of Texas, Ironroot will destroy them. This bourbon is special. This distillery is special, and this family is unlike anyone else in the spirits industry.

"I like to give Kris Hart a hard time when he talks about bourbon having a very finite set of flavors and it being way less complex than scotch. And I'll say that's because we're not playing with all the tools in the chest. If you play around within different grains, different climates, different proofing methods, you can create a whole variety of different flavors that aren't seen in Kentucky bourbon. People are just used to drinking bourbon that's been made in the same place for 300 years," Robert said. Maybe this is your moment to show a bourbon drinking friend of yours what a bourbon can taste like when you strip away all that pesky tradition.

HARBINGER 115

This flagship bourbon has won every award you can think of, including, and most importantly, World's Best Bourbon by *Whisky Magazine* in 2020; , encapsulating everything that defines Ironroot; it is made with purple corn, Bloody Butcher corn, flint corn, non-GMO yellow dent corn, and rye.

PROOF: 115

NOSE: Cinnamon, orange marmalade, blackberry, strawberry compote, brown sugar-maple cookies.

PALATE: Fresh served elote, baking spices, caramel kettle corn, dry, charred oak, nice astringency.

HARBINGER XC

The lighter little brother to Harbinger; made with purple corn, Bloody Butcher corn, flint corn, non-GMO yellow dent corn, and rye.

PROOF: 90

NOSE: Cinnamon candy, maple butter blondies, orange peel, vanilla bean.

PALATE: Bright, dried fruit, black pepper, brown butter maple tart, vanilla pear pie.

PROMETHEAN

This is the "other" bourbon. Intentionally designed to have more of a dried fruit and tobacco vibe, while also being a little more cocktail ready. ; made with red flint corn, non-GMO yellow corn, and rye.

PROOF: 100

NOSE: Vanilla-cream scones with strawberry rhubarb jam, French fig and vanilla slice, baking spices, hint of Cheyenne.

PALATE: Charred corn tortilla, cracked black pepper, plums, toasted oak, savory, coconut and roasted walnuts, long magical finish.

IRONROOT
R
REPUBLIC

IRONROOT
PROMETHEAN
BOURBON WHISKEY

R DENISON

2017 EDITION	103	PROOF
NON-CHILL FILTERED	51.5	% ALC/VOL.
AGED: 16 MONTHS	750	ML

DISTILLED FROM GRAIN IN DENISON, TEXAS

ICARUS

100% corn whiskey finished for an additional year in both port and peated single malt barrels; made with heirloom purple corn, red flint corn, and non-GMO yellow dent corn.

PROOF: 107.2

NOSE: Stewed pears, cream soda, pastry dough, sauteed skillet corn, prunes, light smoke

PALATE: Burnt pupusa, ginger snaps, Band-Aids, salted caramel, cinnamon bark, soft vanilla bean, fennel.

ESOTERIC

Half-bourbon, half-corn whiskey created with the intention of blending it, then bottling half of it and putting back the other half. It's kind of an infinity-style batch. "We wanted to make something that would give us a lot of latitude," said Jonathan. This is going to be an ongoing experiment that only Ironroot would be able to pull off.

PROOF: 97

NOSE: Roasted marshmallow, the white part of a black and white cookie, sugar cookie dough, grilled peaches with black pepper.

PALATE: Steeped black tea, dried cherries, French toast with mixed berry syrup, mango chutney.

THE UNBEARABLE IMPORTANCE OF GRAIN

JONATHAN LIKARISH

For centuries, French brandy makers have cultivated specific varietals of grapes to create their world-class Cognacs and Armagnacs. Their regulations only allow for certain varietals to be used in order to maintain a level of quality, aroma, and taste. If such care is used in the selection of raw materials for brandy production, one would assume it should translate to whiskey as well, but are grains truly important?

The bourbon world has accepted that rye and wheat can be used as "flavoring grains," with the former being a spicy or herbal flavor and the latter providing more sweetness. Of course, the balance of these mash bills are yellow dent corn and distiller's malted barley. The corn is the sugary fuel to produce alcohol, whereas the malt chemically simplifies the sugars to prime them for fermentation. Simply put, would you like your bourbon with rye flavor or wheat flavor? In my experience, very few people can actually differentiate between the two in a blind taste test. There are so many different factors that contribute flavor into a final bourbon expression. Beyond grain, there's water, yeast, fermentation, mashing and distillation techniques, barrels, maturation conditions, and filtration, just to name a few.

What percentage of a whiskey's final flavor comes from grain? Any attempt to quantify this would be extremely subjective at best and nonsensical at worst, because of all the underlying conditions. There are some things that we know for certain. We know that if a grain does not contain the appropriate amount of carbohydrate material, we will be unable to produce the desired amount of alcohol. Whiskey without alcohol isn't really whiskey. The next thing we know is that if the grain is infected by mold or other contaminates, more than likely there will be flavor connotations in the final product. So, grain has already established itself as very important. It provides the sugars for alcohol creation and if those grains aren't high enough quality, it can ruin the final product. But what about flavor?

At Ironroot, we have distilled over forty different varietals of grain, with the bulk of those being different types of corn. The first thing we do with a new type of corn is make corn bread. We do this to get an idea of the different flavors each varietal can bring to the table. Many people have tried yellow corn tortilla chips, and white corn tortilla chips, or blue corn tortilla chips and most people can differentiate between those flavors. Does that flavor difference translate into whiskey? It can, provided it isn't covered up by something else, like oak. It has been widely held in the bourbon industry that corn contributes zero flavor to the final product. Some claim that the distillation process doesn't allow for nuanced corn flavors to come through in the distillate. This is laughable since all of the grains are distilled and rye and wheat are still considered flavoring grains. In reality, there is some merit in the concept of corn having little to no effect on flavor, but the reason has less to do with distillation and more to do with the type of corn selected.

Corn is one of the most manipulated grains in existence. It started as a grass in what is modern day Mexico and was selectively bred gor generations. From there, corn proliferated into other parts of the world where it has been hybridized both by design and accidentally, and most recently became the favorite target of seed companies to genetically modify. As a result of these manipulations, corn has changed dramatically over thousands of years. In order to produce a sweeter corn for eating, corn was hybridized to contain more carbohydrates. In order to produce more ethanol for the fuel industry, corn was modified to produce a greater amount of sugar, and thus more efficiently produce alcohol. In either case, flavor complexity was not necessarily the primary concern. We have distilled both genetically modified (GM) and non-GMO yellow corn. The flavor impact is massive. The whiskey produced with GM corn did not have any faults and had a very pleasant taste, but when we compared the whiskey made from GM corn to the whiskey made from non-GMO corn, there was a much different level of depth and complexity in the latter. If we were to use a highly modified corn in our whiskey, we might see little flavor influence in our final product. Many of the varietals we use in our whiskey are heirloom or non-GMO varietals. We have definitely witnessed a flavor difference between our mash bills. In fact, we generally use a majority of yellow dent corn and a small percentage of some of the other types of corn because they can be overpowering. In essence, we use different types of corn as "flavoring grains."

Grains can be as important in whiskey production as we allow them to be. We can simply use them as fuel for fermentation and cover up their flavors with heavy oak profiles or we can find beauty and nuance in different grains and accentuate them as a Cognac maker would a specific type of grape. Either way, yes: grains are important.

Jonathan Likarish is the master distiller and master blender at Ironroot Republic Distilling Company. In some circles, he's known as the "Ginger" distiller.

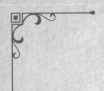

LOCKWOOD DISTILLING COMPANY

LOCKWOOD DISTILLING COMPANY is as much community destination as it is distillery. The food is fantastic, the atmosphere is laid back, and the patio is the best in the neighborhood, just ask a regular. Husband and wife Evan and Sally Batt are the owners and operators of Lockwood and from the beginning the intention was to create a comfortable, family-friendly neighborhood joint. They also happen to make their own spirits.

Prominently painted on one of the walls is "We're just all one big family now," a quote from the band The Revivalists, firmly establishing the familial atmosphere. "My wife and I wanted to do something in our community where people could come celebrate monumental and everyday victories with friends and neighbors. We wanted to build something on our own and were inspired by old distilleries that just produced for their neighborhood, village, town, or simply just their community. We very much believe that you should drink what you like. So, we created a variety of spirits and hope we have something for just about anybody," Evan said.

Lockwood is currently waiting on their own whiskey to age while sourcing their current selections of bourbon and rye from a Central Texas distiller. They also have a fantastic Bourbon Cream that you could easily, and happily, add to every cup of coffee you ever have. Just make sure you save enough for the rest of the family.

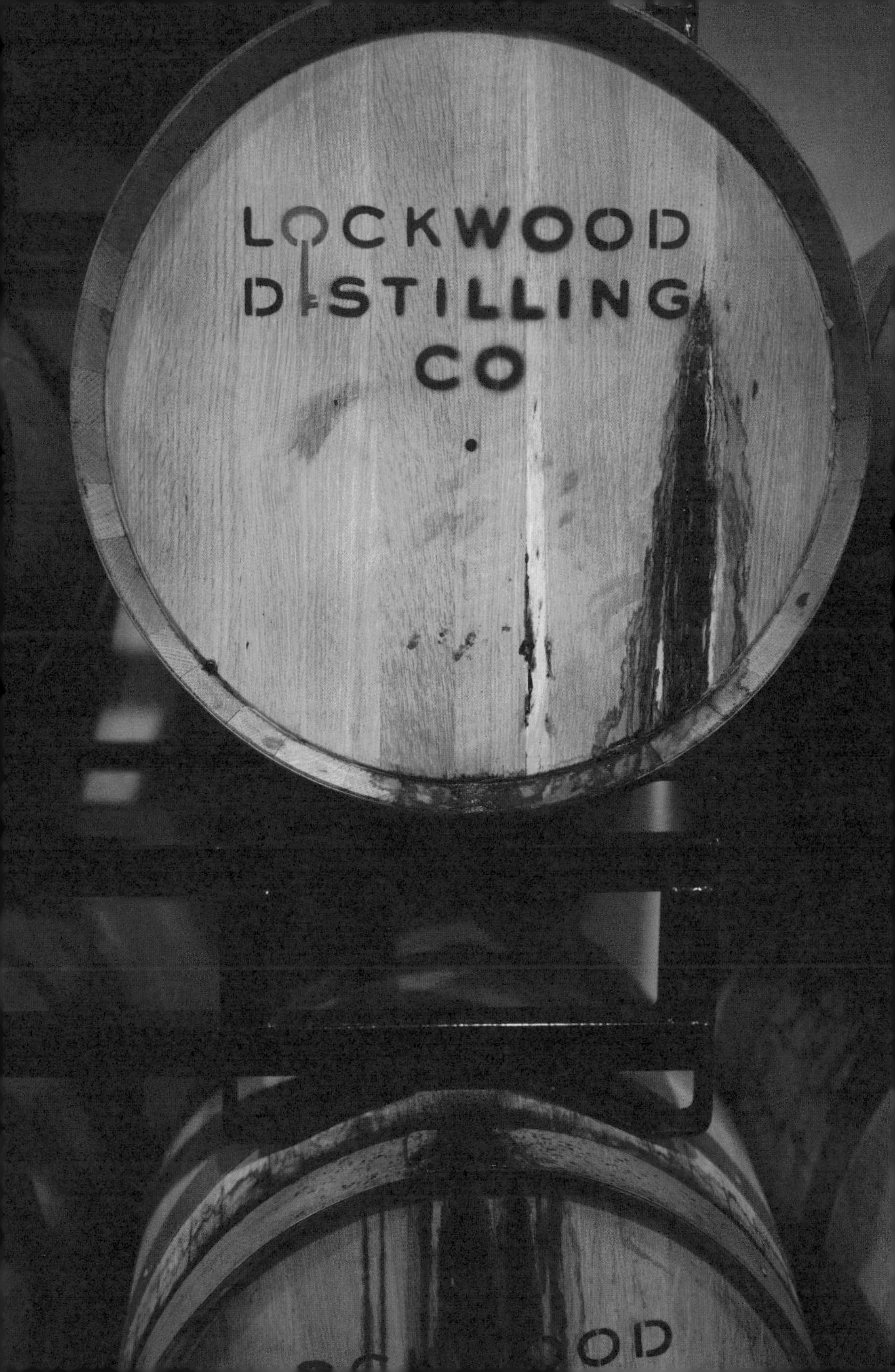
LOCKWOOD
DISTILLING
CO

LOCKWOOD
DISTILLING
CO
.

SINGLE BARREL
STRAIGHT BOURBON WHISKEY
50% ALC/VOL (100 PROOF)
750ML

SINGLE BARREL STRAIGHT BOURBON WHISKEY

This is a sourced Central Texas corn mash with Oklahoma rye; a much more concentrated flavor than their Straight Bourbon Whiskey.

PROOF: 100

NOSE: Almond biscotti, cut vanilla bean, toasted baguette.

PALATE: Molasses, Nilla Wafers, the syrup in the jar when the maraschino cherries are gone, old cork, fortune cookie.

LONE ELM
TX-20007
BARREL: 1223
FILLED ON: 6/13/2020
LOT: 20-F-13-1
DISTILLED FROM GRAIN IN FORNEY, TEXAS

LONE ELM

LET'S KICK THIS OFF WITH A SIMPLE FACT: Forney, Texas, is about as country as you can get, but it's less than twenty minutes from Dallas. Being a resident of the aforementioned massive metropolitan area, no one in Dallas seems to realize this. Whiskey lovers in the greater DFW Metroplex, you have no excuse to not visit Five Points Distilling.

Bill Wofford and his college buddies used to travel extensively to Kentucky, looking for the best of what they could find, seeking out the unicorn bottles they heard so much about. After one particularly disappointing trip (because of the shortages of the whiskey they were looking for), they found themselves sitting around a campfire and, after a few drams, they started talking about how they thought they could make their own whiskey. Usually, these stories end with everyone forgetting the rest of the evening and having accidentally consumed a bottle of Pappy 20, but not these guys. While they intentionally consumed a Pappy 20 that night, Wofford declared that he could make a whiskey just as good and his buddies asked him to prove it. They literally threw money into the pot and that night formed Five Points Distilling (one point for each partner). The first batch of Lone Elm Whiskey was distilled in June 2013. "We knew we were going to make a great whiskey, but we were also better scientists than business guys," Wofford admitted with a laugh.

With a doctorate in physical chemistry from Texas A&M, and having a previous career in semiconductors, Wofford is not your typical distiller (but, I finally have a semiconductor guy). The same as Wofford's uncommon career path, wheat whiskey is an uncommon whiskey. While there are certainly some heavy hitters that make wheated bourbons, Weller and Pappy and Maker's Mark for instance, a true wheat whiskey is pretty unique. "The sweet wheat mash bill is like nothing else in the state. We also take twelve hours to distill and our cuts are very tightly done by taste and smell. We also use smaller barrels, so you have a unique opportunity with our climate to create a very unique flavor profile. The profile is heavy on the oak and vanilla because of the way we use our barrels," Wofford told me.

Lone Elm is entirely grain to glass. From the beginning, the fellas decided they wanted to make a wheat whiskey and they custom-designed their distillery to reflect that. They have also partnered with local farmers to source their red winter wheat and then they give back the spent mash to farmers to fertilize their crops, which, they believe, helps produce a better quality of wheat. They also started their process in a variety of barrel sizes. Always using new white American oak, but they started with 15-gallon barrels, quickly moving to 30-gallon barrels, and now they have plenty of whiskey resting in 53-gallon barrels. This leads to some amazing single barrel picks and some incredible variety of whiskeys for their small-batch blends.

Another thing that makes the whole Lone Elm story even cooler is their head distiller, Logan Miller. This small-town kid from Nebraska is the youngest head distiller in Texas. Hell, he might have been the youngest distiller in the US, at 22, when he started in 2014. While not necessarily convicted of anything, Miller did get a stern talking to when he was caught building his own still in his dorm room in Pomona, California. Now, thankfully, he has access to a real distillery for his experiments.

One of the best anecdotes about Lone Elm came from Kris Hart, the host of Whiskey Neat: "This is what can happen when Texas whiskey stops focusing on the word 'bourbon'. Their wheat whiskey is the best whiskey coming out of the state." I will tell you right now that Lone Elm's Single Barrel Wheat Whiskey is the most underrated whiskey coming out of Texas, without a doubt. If you're looking for that Texas whiskey that no one really knows about right now, but is something that will annihilate better known whiskeys in blind taste tests, this is it.

Congratulations! You found the unicorn. Grab some Lone Elm before the world knows about it, because I promise you that I'm going to do my damnedest to make sure the world does soon.

SMALL BATCH

Aged in 15-gallon American white oak barrels with a #3 char; 90% wheat, 10% malted barley, this is a wheat whiskey, make no bones about it.

PROOF: 90

NOSE: Mixed berry crumble, dried cherry, dates, buttered pound cake with vanilla icing.

PALATE: Raisins, muscovado, dark chocolate covered sea salt caramels, Triscuits with a hint of coriander.

SINGLE BARREL

The single barrel, non-blended version of their small batch aged in 15- gallon American white oak barrels with a #3 char; 90% wheat, 10% malted barley. Don't get scared off by the proof, which varies, because it drinks fairly easily.

PROOF: 126.2

NOSE: Dark cherry, stone fruit, dark berry compote, poached pears with vanilla sauce.

PALATE: Black currant jam, dark Mexican chocolate, boot leather and a touch of pipe tobacco, finishing with vanilla.

OLOROSO SHERRY CASK FINISHED STRAIGHT WHEAT WHISKEY

The traditional Lone Elm Small Batch finished in an Oloroso sherry cask. This is currently distillery only in 375ml bottles, but there are plans for distribution. I'm a huge fan of finished whiskey, and I have to tell you, this whiskey is simply fantastic.

 PROOF: 123.3

 NOSE: Ripe plums, sugar-soaked dates, hints of pipe tobacco and fresh buttered biscuits.

 PALATE: Chocolate-covered cherries, sweet caramel, with a bit of licorice, pecans, and toffee.

I WOULD BAKE, FOR WILLIE NELSON

Ariel Wakeland has been a member of the United States Bartenders' Guild since 2018 and joined the board in 2019. Wakeland still remembers her first sip of Lone Elm, sitting outside on a day when fall was starting to feel tangible. For her, it's a sweet and smooth whiskey that doesn't need to be dressed up, but knows how to show up at a party. She loves whiskey in her sweet tea, as this cocktail, inspired a little by Willie and a little by Beyoncé, makes clear.

2 oz. Fat-Washed Lone Elm Whiskey

1 oz. cold brew black tea

1 dash walnut bitters

1. Add all of the ingredients to a mixing glass filled with ice, stir, and strain into a rocks glass over a large ice cube.

2. Sip, and imagine Willie Nelson is sitting with you, telling stories about eating pie.

Fat-Washed Lone Elm Whiskey: Add 1 stick of unsalted butter to a saucepan over medium heat. Slowly melt the butter until it just begins to brown. Pour the melted butter into a bowl and, using the same saucepan, toast equal parts chopped pecans and shredded coconut, cooking for a few minutes to release their oils. Add the toasted pecans and coconut to the butter and then pour 16 oz. Lone Elm Whiskey into the bowl. Stir well, transfer to an airtight container, and let cool for a couple hours before freezing for 24 hours. Remove the container from the freezer and strain.

MBS SEED

CHRIS GARCIA

MBS Seed has been selling seed to Texas farmers and ranchers since 1989. Several years ago, I was approached by a local distiller looking for locally sourced grains, and that was my introduction into the world of Texas whiskey. Since we were selling seed to Texas farmers, we already had the types of grain needed on hand. Grain and seed are the same physical structure; the only difference being that as seed, it is being planted to germinate and grow a plant. As a grain, it will be processed strictly for its physical properties and doesn't necessarily need to have specific germination characteristics. So, we were already selling seed to farmers and ranchers that could also be used as grain for distillation.

There was a bit of a learning curve as I found out what characteristics make the best grain for distilling. The things that make the seed best for planting aren't always the same things that make it the best for distilling. Weather, soil, fertility, and crop management have a lot of impact on grain quality, and as I learned what characteristics were most desirable in grain for distilling, I was able to select the crop that had the best growing conditions and crop management during that season. Since we were already selling the seed to the farmers, I could watch as the growing season progressed and then select grain from the areas that had optimum rainfall at the right times, were dry during the right times, etc., which would yield the right specs needed for distilling.

We have had some distillers ask for one specific field that could be their grain source, in order to have that aspect of their story, but having only one location that you depend on for your grain is extremely risky. If that field gets too little rain during the time the grain is filling, it will have low starch content, which means low alcohol production. If it gets too much rain at or before harvest, the grain may start sprouting in the head, or could develop fungal or mold issues. And ultimately, it only takes one spring hail storm to wipe out that field. If all your eggs are in that one basket, then you are stuck with whatever grain is produced, which could be low yields, not enough grain to meet demand, flavors and smells that are off, etc. That's why we select grain from the area that has the best quality for producing the highest quality flavors and yields for our customers.

We also bought a roller mill and a hammer mill so we could mill and bag grain to customers' exact specs. There's been a lot of trial and error, lessons learned from experience and help from others in the industry to figure out how to offer the right product in the right way to the distillers. Working in the distilling industry is definitely a different environment than our seed customers. There are different considerations, timelines, and needs, but we strive every day to get better at it and offer quick, custom service to our distillers with grain that fits their specific needs.

We are currently working on some Texas heirloom corns for production, as well as working with a corn breeder to select conventional yellow dent corns that have more optimum flavors and distilling specs. We are always looking at other processes for changing grain characteristics and are experimenting with ways to bring out flavors and make starch break down easier.

Most importantly, I love working with the Texas distillers. I love being a part of their creations and their stories. It's not often you can come in at the ground floor of a fledgling industry and get to be a small part of the story as it grows and flourishes. All of us at MBS Seed love this part of the business. We've become whiskey buffs/fans/snobs over the last few years, enjoying the opportunity to taste the spirits that started out as our grain. It's such a small part of the complex and truly artistic process of creating whiskey, but we are humbled to play our small role in it.

MBS Seed is located in Denton, Texas, and specializes in range and pasture grass seed, hybrid sorghums and field seed, lawn grasses, legumes, wildlife seed, and vegetable seed. Chris Garcia is a founding partner.

SILVER STAR SPIRITS

WHEN I WAS A KID, I remember staring out the window as we cruised down I-30, heading to my Welita's house in Fort Worth. Every time I'd see this huge building on the outskirts of town and I'd tell my mom or brother or whoever's attention I could grab "that's where the beans come from." The Ranch Style beans factory, originally built in 1932, has been a part of Fort Worth for almost a century.

In 2011, a very large portion of the former bean plant was converted into Trinity River Distilling. Now Silver Star Spirits, the scope of the distillery itself is one of the more impressive in the state. Their tasting room is beautiful and they host live music at their massive outdoor party every weekend. If you're there for a tour, hope you get one of the volunteers who used to work there when they were still cranking out legumes.

Silver Star Whiskey is made with rainwater. With the expansion of their barrel room and the addition of Kirk Richards as a new part owner and full-time distiller, Silver Star is finally getting into additional flavor profiles like rye and single malt. Moving away from previous whiskeys that involved the use of NGS, this version of Silver Star seems to be more thoughtful and more crafty than previous leadership teams had been. With multiple column stills and hybrid pot stills, they have the ability to go in several interesting directions in the not too distant future. Hopefully at least one of them is "ranch style."

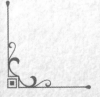

TEXAS SILVER STAR STRAIGHT BOURBON WHISKEY

This expression is a welcome departure from other whiskeys made by former owners of the company; it is made with corn, rye, and barley and aged in 30-gallon white oak barrels for just over 3 years.

PROOF: 90

NOSE: Caramel syrup, vanilla beans, grilled corn on the cob, cooking oil.

PALATE: Cabbage, hay-filled barn, cream soda, maple with a slight white pepper and chocolate finish.

SILVER STAR

1849

STRAIGHT BOURBON WHISKEY

45% ALC. BY VOL. (90 Proof) 750 ml

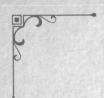

TAHWAHKARO

ONE OF THE THINGS I'VE LOVED THE MOST about putting this book together is getting to know the wonderful people in this industry and hearing their stories. Most of those stories have something to do with a decision that was made by a bunch of folks who had the desire but not the specific knowledge to jump headfirst into distilling. Tahwahkaro is one of the only distilleries in Texas that has a bit of distilling in their family history, but it was a tragedy that led to its inception.

Justin Jackson suffered a tragic car accident in 2012. "My wife and I had just left our mother's funeral. I don't remember this, but I've been told that we were stuck behind an 18-wheeler when we were hit by another truck and I lost my wife immediately. I woke up in the hospital three days later and I had lost the two most important women in my life in one week. I got out three weeks later and I needed to restart . . . Life, you know?" Justin told me. "I started making whiskey because my brother was making whiskey. He's one of the owners of Axe & Oak Distilling Company out of Colorado Springs."

Justin spent some time in Colorado with his brother Jason. After a few months, he decided to move to Dallas to be closer to his wife's family. "I was on the phone with my brother every day, but once we got the equipment, a year and a half later, we dedicated ourselves to making 100% grain-to-glass whiskey. Never sourcing," said Justin. He's an artist. The real reason he's a distiller, beyond jumping at the opportunity to work with his brother, is that he's a creator. "The artistry side of distilling is all about how to balance all those pieces of the mash bill." He told me that it was always important for them to maintain their commitment to grain to glass, which is what the craft movement should be all about. "It's important for us to make every drop ourselves," Justin told me.

The brothers began distilling in 2017 and their first product was released in 2019. In fact, the first drops of the first batch that came out of Tawahkaro were submitted to the East Texas Shoot Out, hosted by the infamous Jim Murray. Since then, their Tahwahkaro Barrel Strength Bourbon took home a silver medal at the San Francisco World Spirits Competition.

Jason is thrilled to have relocated to Texas and to be dedicated to making 100% Texas whiskey with his brother. "Before I moved down, a friend of mine told me Texans were the nicest people you'd ever met, but we'll also punch you in the mouth if we have to. I love that mindset." Now with that, I can agree, but I'd much rather share a dram with y'all than to punch anyone in the mouth... unless you lie on your label. Seriously. In the mouth. Don't lie to a Texan.

TEXAS RYE MALT

This is 68% Texas malted rye, 17% Texas Elbon rye berry, 6% Texas yellow corn, 6% Texas red wheat, and 3% Texas two-row barley malt.

PROOF: 105

NOSE: Fresh rye bread, vanilla, heavy barrel notes but rounded, Andes Chocolate Mints.

PALATE: Toffee, rye spice, pepper, hot rye sourdough, very slightly oak tannins, a mint chocolate malt from Dairy Queen vibe.

TAHWAHKARO®

TEXAS RYE MALT WHISKEY

HANDCRAFTED FROM GRAIN TO GLASS

TRADE

TAH
WAHKARO®

MARK

BATCH _____ DISTILLER _____

750 ML

CRAFTED & BOTTLED IN
GRAPEVINE, TEXAS

52.5% ALC/VOL. (105 PROOF)

TAHWAHKARO®

FOUR GRAIN BOURBON WHISKEY

HANDCRAFTED FROM GRAIN TO GLASS

TRADE

MARK

BATCH 8   DISTILLER

750 ML

CRAFTED & BOTTLED IN
GRAPEVINE, TEXAS

48% ALC./VOL. (96 PROOF)

FOUR GRAIN
BOURBON WHISKEY

This is 65% Texas yellow corn, 11% Texas red wheat, 11% Texas Elbon rye berry, 13% of three different types of Texas malt.

PROOF: 96

NOSE: Light and sweet, honey butter, fresh biscuits, blossoming honeysuckle.

PALATE: Slight smoke, corn bread, green pepper, plum, fresh cracked vanilla cream soda.

FOUR GRAIN BOURBON WHISKEY BARREL STRENGTH

Same mash bill as the Four Grain Bourbon; proof may vary and while it's nice and intense, it's not overbearing. The barrel proof brings out the aromatics.

PROOF: 124

NOSE: Waffles served to a kindergartner who's allowed to have as much syrup as they want, gingerbread, buttered skillet corn.

PALATE: Sweet, but more maple syrup than the 96 proof, warm, white pepper, corn casserole, molasses.

TAHWAHKARO ®

FOUR GRAIN BOURBON WHISKEY

BARREL STRENGTH

TRADE

TAH
WAHKARO

MARK

BARREL 18-0010 DISTILLER

750 ML

CRAFTED & BOTTLED IN

GRAPEVINE, TEXAS

62 ALC./VOL (124 PROOF)

TEXMALT

TexMalt, located in Fort Worth, started just like any great idea, over a beer. After a long work week, founders Austin Schumacher and Chase Leftwich were visiting one of their local breweries when they asked the head brewer, "Where does your malt come from?" At the time, the answer was that there was no source for local malted grains and the closest source was a large corporate malting facility 1,500 miles away. To Schumacher and Leftwich, this was unacceptable because they personally knew Texas farming families located much closer. They knew quality malting barley and other grains could be grown locally and they became determined to make it a reality.

Schumacher and Leftwich went to work learning the malting process and eventually attended the Canadian Malting Barley Technical Center in Winnipeg. At the same, time they began working closely with their Texas farmers to grow special varieties of malting barley and other brewing and distilling grains suited for the Texas environment.

In the summer of 2016 TexMalt had malted and sold its very first batch of malting barley made on a small floor malting operation capable of yielding a half-ton batch. Today, TexMalt offers small-batch floor malting along with their precision-controlled Germination Box capable of producing over eight tons per week.

Currently, the brewing and distilling grain market is dominated by large-scale producers in the Northern United States and Europe, shipping millions of pounds of malted products to every continent. These mass operations require grain to be purchased on a global-commodities market and shipped thousands of miles. As a result, an enormous amount of fossil fuel, water, and petrochemicals is used to produce a majority of the grains found in craft beer and spirits.

TexMalt has grown to be the regional alternative to these practices. They work closely with their partner farms to implement the most environmentally sound practices possible. By connecting local and regional brewers and distillers with regional farmers, they reduce the average number of food miles associated with each batch of malt or grain to around 300 miles instead of up to 3,000 miles. That equates to a reduction of 4.5 tons of carbon emissions on average for every truckload of grain.

Schumacher and Leftwich started with the idea of connecting Texas farms with Texas breweries and distilleries. Today, the malt and grains that TexMalt offers far surpass any large-scale operation due to the hard work and local relationships that were built. TexMalt will always strive to offer the best ingredients so their customers can make the best beer and spirits possible.

THE MALTING PROCESS

BLAZE MAY

Seeing grain that you have grown yourself in the vast expanse of the Texas Panhandle, malted at your facility, and then seeing it become a Texas spirit is one of the most satisfying things I've had the pleasure to be a part of. From a farmer's perspective, seeing the grain change into a completely different product using nature's chemistry is still fascinating. Highly scientific while intensely intuitive, simply put, most of malting is a controlled sprouting of the grain. We guide every kernel through the process so it becomes what we want, then use man's first discovery, fire, to mold the grain and preserve what was created during the sprouting. Below is a more in-depth look at what was discovered (I like to think man's second discovery) many thousands of years ago and perfected into the process we see today.

Steeping is where the grain starts this journey. Fundamentally, it is a simple idea. Soak the grain in water until it sprouts. In practice, this is a challenging proposition and arguably the most important step in the process. The goal is to sprout all of the grain within hours of each other. If you were to plant that same grain in the field, it would sprout over a period of two weeks or more. To malt a consistent product, the uniformity is a must: too warm of water and the kernels sprout at an inconsistent pace; if it's too cold, however, some may not sprout at all. The amount of moisture absorbed into each kernel during the steep will determine how well the grain performs in the following steps. We also need to control the uptake of oxygen, the extraction of CO_2, and the removal of any dirt and contaminants that might make a good malt go south. Once we have control of the grain through the steep the next step, germination, will proceed much easier.

Germination continues the natural process of a seed. Only now will we start to see the modification and enzyme creation. For this step to continue properly and consistently we add humid cool air to the grain bed, keeping every kernel growing in a consistent and controlled manner while adding oxygen and removing CO_2. The now sprouted grain begins to grow a small plant as well as small roots or rootlets. To prevent the rootlets from matting together, we have to periodically agitate the grain. As the plant and roots first start growing, stored energy is needed. Enzymes are created that convert the grain's starch into sugars the plant can use to continue growing. This modification of the starch is what the maltster is going for, in addition to enzyme production. The sugars are what yeast loves to feast on while the enzymes created continue to break down the starch. In a distiller's malt, there are enough enzymes to not only self-convert its own starch, but also to convert starch in the rest of the raw grains in the mash bill. After our analysis, as long as the grain has modified properly, we then move to step three, introducing fire.

Kilning the grain is where we preserve what has been created by drying the grain to a low moisture content. The enzymes become dormant and shelf life is extended. This is when we create something more than what nature provided us. Also, we can manipulate the relative humidity, speed, and temperature of the air we are putting on the grain to create an assortment of flavors and aromas. We create specific tasting notes of varying fruits, caramels, and toasty flavors that can add complexity to any distillate. This, in turn, allows us to provide a wide variety of products for whatever a distiller might need.

Malting grain that we have grown ourselves here in Wildorado, Texas, adding value to an undervalued commodity, and seeing it used in many different and fantastic spirits, has been a wonderful experience. We are excited for the future and our craft.

Blaze May is the co-founder, along with Cory Athro, of Maverick Malt House, which is located in Wildorado.

CENTRAL TEXAS ★

CENTRAL TEXAS

CENTRAL TEXAS IS THE HEART OF THE STATE. When my great grandfather came to Texas with only his family's wagon and a little bit of hope, he settled in a place called Brady, now known as the "Heart of Texas," as it's smack dab in the middle of the state. Central Texas has always encompassed a collection of all of the things that make up Texas. No coast, no mountains, but this region is the epitome of the great South Plains. Here you'll find some of the largest facilities in the state (Balcones, Still Austin) and some of the smallest (Banner, Spirit of Texas) and, without question, the best barbecue on the planet. Shout out to my cousins in Kansas City who are going to be mad about that one, bless your hearts.

AUSTIN 101

"WE LAUNCHED OUR COMPANY IN THE MIDDLE OF A PANDEMIC" is a phrase that will, no doubt, become a part of the origin story for countless businesses across the world. The first chapter in Austin 101's story wasn't exactly what founders Stephan Godevais, Gary Kotshott, and Tom Buchsbaum had in mind, but they're more than happy to own it. "Even though it was unlucky to launch then," said Godevais, "we were very lucky that the Texas Whiskey Festival had just happened."

There were over 1,000 people at the 2020 Texas Whiskey Festival and Austin 101 won second place in the People's Choice voting. They received their first order from their distributor right after the event and it was five times the size they were expecting. It's an uphill battle to launch a new product with little history and I can't imagine how they felt about facing that hill without the ability to share samples with consumers at liquor stores or to have any launch events at restaurants. The pandemic had a major impact on the craft segment of the spirits industry, primarily because of the inability to market products through the traditional channels. More spirits were sold, sure, but those brands that saw an increase in sales were already familiar to consumers.

Austin 101 is sourcing their whiskey from another Austin-based distiller, but it is a 100% grain-to-glass Texas whiskey. It's interesting how it's becoming more and more possible to source Texas whiskey. This creates opportunity for more upstarts like Austin 101, who wanted a Texas product, but also wanted to source.

Now, what exactly is a light whiskey and why would you make one? Light whiskey only has one rule: the whiskey must be pulled from the still above 160 proof and below 190 proof. Austin 101 is barreled at 125 proof, aged for 101 days in 25-gallon barrels (mostly ex-Garrison Brothers bourbon barrels), and bottled at 101 proof.

AUSTIN 101 LIGHT WHISKEY

Light whiskey, aged 101 days in used American oak barrels, all
Texas grains: white corn, malted barley, red wheat.

PROOF: 101

NOSE: Salted butterscotch blondies,
fresh corn on the cob, ethanol, hay.

PALATE: Werther's Original, creamed
corn, light vanilla pudding, longer
finish than expected.

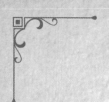

BALCONES

OF ALL OF THESE PROFILES, Balcones was the one that took the longest to figure out. Truthfully, I'm not sure if I can even quite cover it all, but I'll do my damnedest. Balcones, to me, is the personification of everything that's happening in the Texas whiskey industry. Balcones is the bell of the Texas whiskey ball.

Founded by Chip Tate and Jared Himstedt in 2008, Balcones released the first Texas whiskey to market. Just to clarify, although this truly only matters to a very small handful of people, Garrison Brothers was the first distillery in Texas to make whiskey, and the first distillery to release a bourbon, but Balcones was the first distillery in Texas to release a Texas whiskey.

Balcones started its distillery in a former welding shop under an overpass in Waco, with stills they procured from Portugal. Today, they find themselves in the 65,000-square-foot historic Texas Fireproof Storage building in downtown Waco, with enough capacity to make over 800,000 liters of spirits a year. They currently use two wash stills and two spirit stills from Forsyths in Scotland, and custom designed the stills with exceptionally long necks and an upward sloping Lynn arm, to prolong the amount of copper contact.

Balcones' volatile relationship with their former founding member has been well documented and I'm sure it will make an incredible film one day. If you would like to know more, feel free to toss his name into a search engine with the word "lawsuit" and you'll find plenty. That, however, is not the goal of this book. That, my friends, is not what matters most about Balcones.

"When we started, Baby Blue was the first thing we released," said Himstedt, head (not master) distiller at Balcones. When they started the distillery, it was to make single malt. They were piecing together a whole bunch of equipment that wasn't really meant for fermentation. "Our mash tun was damaged, but we realized that basically everything else in the distillery was good to go, so we could do everything besides barley. It started as more of a hypothesis than anything. Most

Est. 1912
World Cooperage

BALCONES
D I S T I L L I N G

Profile Series

American Oak
36 Months Extra Fine Grain
Profile 61 YS

classic American whiskey styles are so wood forward. You can hear Jimmy Russell or Jim Rutledge talk and they're going to say somewhere between 60 to 80 percent of the final whiskey is wood contributions. So we wanted to see what would happen if we treated our corn distillate with more of a Speyside-style approach. Could we do something a little more subtle, elegant, and fruity with more nuance? And because we wanted to showcase the grain, we wanted to be a little more particular with the selection."

Ultimately, the selection was local, Central Texas blue corn. This was the beginning of Balcones commitment to an entirely grain-to-glass distillery. For Balcones' ingredients come first. They use predominantly two grain types, a malted barley called Golden Promise, a very well-known Scottish barley that is very sweet and biscuity, and heirloom corn instead of yellow dent #2. They use Texas-grown blue corn that they roast to make it more bright and buttery, as well as getting rid of the flinty, off flavors. Balcones uses a scotch malt whiskey yeast for almost every product, as well as English ale yeast for some added complexity.

Part of the distillery expansion a few years ago was the building of an additional rickhouse outside of town. "We have about 2,000 barrels here and about 11,000 outside the city limits," said Himstedt. I asked if there was a discernible difference between the two and he said it was huge, explaining how the wood impact was much slower out there than in town. "That's not a bad thing. It's actually great. We're kinda having to work backward and we're trying to figure out how to slow down the aging process so we can make older whiskey without it becoming over-wooded."

Their single malt expressions are being housed downtown, and they have recently acquired 500-600L barrels, which they are going to use to get their whiskey to 8 to 12 years, an absolute first for any Texas spirit. Himstedt said, "We wanted to see, between entry proof and barrel size, if we can even do an 8 to 10 to 12 year that's still delicate but more mature. Those are all European wine barrels, so we talked to Independent Stave and agreed that if we like it, they would make a new American oak version," which would allow them to use them for bourbon.

In 2016, Independent Stave began construction on their Research Center, easily making them the most innovative American cooperage. From their press release: "We are looking at all the elements to build a barrel—oak species, wood age, barrel shape and size, how we engineer the barrels, all the materials used —to optimize the barrels we craft." Andrew Wiehebrink, ISC Director of Spirit

Research and Innovation, confirmed this: "We encourage distillers to bring us their ideas and challenges. We know how to transform ideas into reality, with sensory and science-backed results."

"We're not the only reason they have it," said Himstedt, "but the whole research department didn't exist before us and when they were forming it, they're like, 'Hey, we've hired a wood science guy to run our new R&D department and a lot of it had to do with questions you've been asking.' They realized they couldn't answer us because they didn't have the supporting science. During his first week on the job, he came down here to hang out for a few days, tasting stuff in the warehouse, jotting down notes. He had some cool ideas, like directly peating barrels." The plan was to char new American oak barrels with peat from various places across the globe. Apparently Himstedt was trying to make a barrel that would create a Dr. Pepper flavor in the wood extraction. "Man, if you can give me a barrel that's going to taste like Dr. Pepper and I'm in Waco. I mean, come on..." I, personally, hope it's a tad closer to the aspartame vibe of Diet Dr. Pepper because I have consumed as much of that writing this thing as I have whiskey. Seriously. I have a problem.

Fun Fact: Himstedt may be a barrel nerd, but he's far more of a traditionalist than you'd expect from someone this creative. "I'm really hesitant to do rye or bourbon in finishing barrels, because there's a longstanding tradition not to, but single malt? Absolutely, no brainer.

"Regarding the barrels, early on, we did everything we could, to take advantage of how the climate could go. We exclusively used 5-gallon barrels up until 2013, but now all our barrels are all custom and they're 59 gallons. When we started asking all those questions and no one could answer them, they transferred us to the wine team and now they make our barrels on the wine line." Currently, the biggest challenge is increasing the amount of time in the barrel, to take advantage of those changes in whiskey that can only truly be achieved with time, but keeping the impact of the Texas heat at bay, so they're also playing around with the level of extractives in their barrels.

Here's something interesting happening in Texas whiskey that feels like it could be the "next big thing." There are multiple Texas distillers, with Balcones and Ironroot leading the way, playing around with single-grain recipes. Think about it as deconstructed bourbon. Instead of the mash bill being corn, rye, and wheat all cooked together, they make a corn distillate, a rye distillate, and a wheat distillate and blend it after aging. The art of blending is becoming one of the most interesting elements in American whiskey today and these distillers are giving themselves the opportunity to make whiskeys with even greater precision. "Our Pot Still [Bourbon] is made that way. We have a wheated recipe, a high-rye recipe, a 2-grain that's malt and blue corn, and a 100% blue corn and the Pot Still Bourbon is a hybrid of those. Even the production guys are like 'Hey man... once you figure out what your ratios are... can we just... make it?" Himstedt laughed.

Scottish single malt traditions were the first beliefs Balcones gravitated toward, including how they named themselves. The Balcones fault line is the longest dormant fault line in North America, hasn't moved in about 50 million years, and runs right underneath I-35 through Texas. If that sucker ever wakes up, we're screwed. "I personally like the idea of not putting the people front and center, and we don't have a great-great grandfather's recipe to base anything on and no old, dead white guy to name ourselves after. There's something about the way that the Scottish names ring and I love that, no matter how fancy they sound, they usually just mean something like 'by the lake.' There's something about that style that felt a little bit more like what we were going to do. When we started, we had no idea what the climate was going to do, we didn't know what the microflora [in the fermentation] was going to do, and we just kinda didn't know how this was going to work here. Because of the environment, it seemed more appropriate that we paid homage to our place of origin rather than naming it after some dudes."

As expected, we wound up having more of a philosophical chat than anything. I asked about the Texas whiskey community as a whole and Himstedt said, "We've all been newbies at some point. I think, right now, the more generous side of the whiskey community is inviting people in and I just want to say, 'Man, you have no idea how this has given me so much joy in my life. I want that to be there for you. And for that to happen, you'll have to try a lot of things and you'll need a desire to learn, but, eventually you're going to wake up and it's going to click. I want that for you.' It happened to me, and I've watched it happen to others and it's a great thing," said Himstedt. "What I can't stand is weaponization of whiskey knowledge. That's not helpful."

The educational aspects of Balcones are some of the most important to the Texas whiskey industry. Not only can you tour the facility and get answers to questions you have, but Balcones is constantly doing blending classes and seminars. The Whisky Talk series they do with radio hosts Ben & Skin has some of my

favorite consumer-facing conversations about their process. They want to grow the category by any means necessary and over the past couple of years they've taken this mindset and literally created products with that in mind. These aren't dumbed down, but they are more entry-level and attainable. Himstedt told me this story about going to a friend's house and commenting on all of the Balcones bottles. When his friend told Himstedt that those were all from his volunteer shifts at the distillery and he wouldn't have been able to afford that many on his social worker salary, it broke Himstedt's heart. The Pot Still Bourbon and their new Lineage Single Malts are made specifically to be more approachable in terms of both flavor profile and price point.

"The last thing I ever wanted was to be making whiskey that my friends can't afford," said Himstedt. "We'll never make something that's zero challenge, because then you'd never progress. But if we can figure out where some of our consumers are starting, we can help them move just one or two steps past it. Especially with my interest in the American single malt category, I'm always trying to figure out ways to get someone who doesn't drink scotch to realize American single malts are an entirely different category. We strive to find ways to have that conversation." The whiskey drinkers of today are far more experimental than they were ten years ago. That conversation is much easier to have now than it was when Balcones began. "There will always be baggage around Kentucky versus Texas, but, ironically, there hasn't been much of that from Scotch and Irish makers. Scotland and Ireland have been more embracing of the global single malt phenomenon than Kentucky has ever been about the proliferation of bourbon. European distillers are super happy about Asian and American single malts and genuinely want the conversation to broaden. They want single malt in other parts of the world to see how they contribute to the category, and it blows my mind. Honestly, that's how everyone should be."

In 2019, Icons of Whisky awarded Himstedt the Master Distiller of the Year award. The irony is that he refuses to be called master distiller. "I struggle with the idea on a lot of levels. On the joking side, I'm not nearly old enough to be a master distiller. I know a lot of the guys that are legendary Hall of Famers and I just wouldn't put myself in that kind of company. In the US, we don't have any official kind of apprentice or journeyman program for craft distilling. We're just a ragtag group of guys who are self taught and never worked in distilling before and just started throwing whiskey out into the world, hoping that people will buy it. This isn't false humility, I mean I know a few things, but there's so much more that I don't know and so much that I have to figure out and that, to me..." he sort of tapered off, so I'll finish the sentence for him... that's a title he doesn't feel like he has yet earned. That's a title reserved for whiskey makers with distilleries older than thirteen years old and distillers old enough to have their names on bottles. Himstedt is too focused on creating interesting products and finding new ways to feed his creativity in order to better himself as a whiskey maker. He'll embrace it one day, but, ironically, that will be around the time he's tired of actually running the stills.

When asked about his inspirations, he said it had a lot to do with the legendary Jim McEwan, who started working at the Bowmore Distillery in 1963 as an apprentice cooper. McEwan then moved to cellar master in the mid '70s, then mastered blending at a large blending house he managed and then, eventually, wound up back at Bowmore. In 2000, he was approached to help revamp the Bruichladdich Distillery. Now, y'all, that is a master distiller. "Some of the first whiskey I ever had were some of his cask experimentations. I loved the lighter peat levels and it being cask strength. The Dusk Voyage series was amazing," Himstedt said.

A lot of people don't know this, but Himstedt also designs all of the labels for the distillery, start to finish. "I do a lot of black on black. It always reminds me of the Misfits' crimson ghost logo and how you'd see it all the time without the name of the band anywhere near it. You wind up with this 'if you know, you know' kind of vibe to it. It's not really meant for marketing, it's meant for people who know what's up and there's something understated about it that I kind of like." Himstedt said he doesn't really have a favorite label, but the use of red with black and gold foil, which you can see on the majority of their single malt products, is "super dope."

The sheer amount of product that Balcones makes now is astonishing. There are currently around twenty releases every year and the law in Texas making it illegal for a distillery to sell a consumer more than two bottles of spirit a month is the main reason Balcones doesn't release more. Balcones has some incredibly cool projects coming down the pike and, thankfully, they're in a financial position where they can release weird whiskey just for the sake of it being weird.

By definition, Texas whiskey is rooted in nascency. It had never been done. "You can claim to be a traditionalist, but we have whiskey maturing in a way that's literally never happened before. And that can be part of how you present yourself or you can present yourself as if you have it all figured out, but to me that's a smokescreen. To me, we're going to spend the next couple, or few, decades, however long it takes, to figure out what our native whiskey should be. I don't want to anthropomorphize the weather, but we need to figure out what kind of whiskey this climate wants to make," said Himstedt. "I hope our collective voice and vibe and the things that we're doing contribute to the overall body of knowledge around whiskey. We say things like 'conversation' or 'narrative' and they seem trite, but the way we interact with consumers is a specific dynamic and we want a feedback loop between producers and consumers. The world of whiskey has exploded so much and between ingredients, process of maturation, and location, there is great whiskey being made today that did not exist twenty years ago. If you think everything new is trash because you're a traditionalist, that's fine, but I don't buy it. My whiskey world is better because people are taking chances and making whiskey in places that are new."

Jared Himstedt concluded, "Making whiskey in Texas is unlike anything else, it has its own personality. Texas whiskey isn't necessarily a class type, but it's a genre. And to think that we were there, getting started as it got started... Looking back in twenty years thinking about how thirty years ago this didn't exist...That's going to be fun."

TEXAS "1" SINGLE MALT

This is the flagship. This is the reason Balcones makes whiskey. If you want a sense of them, this is where you turn. That's why they call it "The One."

PROOF: 106

NOSE: Almond buttercrunch, over-ripe cherries, cocoa powder, banana bread, malted milk balls, but only after you bite them in half.

PALATE: Toasted malt, spicy and dry, Tupelo honey, caramelized pears, a long finish of cinnamon and clove, menthol cigarette mouthfeel.

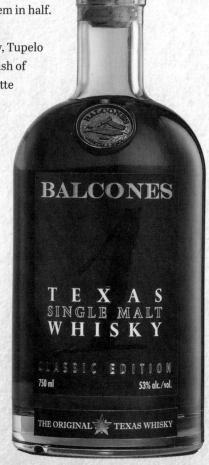

BABY BLUE

The first Texas whiskey on the market since Prohibition; made from roasted heirloom blue corn and is always intentionally young. This sucker has won more awards than Michael Phelps.

PROOF: 92

NOSE: Kettle corn, vanilla cream puff, toffee, cinnamon and nutmeg, French-pressed coffee, 85% chocolate.

PALATE: Oily, dried apricot, brown sugar, cotton candy, sweet tea, warm long slight peppermint, and Sichuan peppers.

BRIMSTONE

This is Baby Blue, but then smoked using Texas scrub oak. It's almost a Texas-style Peat Monster. My favorite thing about Brimstone is that the process is covered by an NDA and everyone at Balcones has to sign it, but then, when they say "Okay! Do you want to know how we do it?" the response is usually, "Nah... I'll probably have too much whiskey one night and tell everyone so, nope, don't tell me."

PROOF: 106

NOSE: Smitty's in Lockhart, freshly picked corn, powdered sugar, peaches graham crackers.

PALATE: Smoked sugar, pipe tobacco, melted butter, orange marmalade, hint of bacon, sweet tea, Mexican chili peppers, long dry finish that ends, unsurprisingly, with smoke.

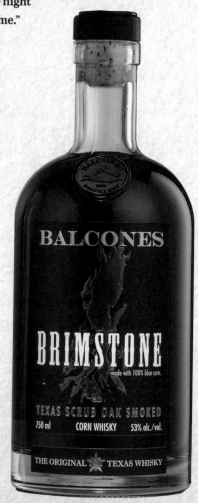

TRUE BLUE CASK
SINGLE BARREL

This is a barrel proof version of True Blue 100, made with roasted blue corn; proof varies. Add a little water if you want to bring out the baking spices and the cocoa powder.

PROOF: 132

NOSE: Fresh baked brioche, grapefruit soda, flambeed banana, pecan pralines, honeysuckle.

PALATE: Roasted pecans, buttered toast, raw honey, coffee cake banana bread, slightly medicinal, long finish with hints of cinnamon.

MIDNIGHT RAMBLER

Chad Solomon and Christy Pope, co-founders of Cuffs & Buttons, were tasked to help create the cocktail program at Midnight Rambler in Dallas. They thought about how not many (if any) house cocktails today are named for the establishment, such as was common in the late 19th century with the Pegu Club cocktail, Clover Club cocktail, and Sazerac, among others. This drink honors the bar that Midnight Rambler has evolved to be thus far over its first five years, featuring flavors and products reflective of the bar and its hometown of Dallas.

2 oz. Balcones TX Pot Still Bourbon

2½ teaspoons Ancho Reyes

½ teaspoon demerara rich syrup (2:1)

1 dash Bittermens Xocolatl Mole Bitters

1 dash Angostura Bitters

2 drops mineral saline

1. Combine all of the ingredients, except the grapefruit twist, in a mixing glass with ice, stir, and strain into a double Old Fashioned glass over a large ice cube. Garnish with a grapefruit twist.

POT STILL BOURBON

Huge. This drinks more like a hot, peppery rye than a bourbon; mash bill consists of their signature blue corn, Texas wheat, rye, and malted barley. There are some big flavors here and if you're not ready for it, that's okay… take a deep breath and try it again. You'll be okay.

PROOF: 92

NOSE: Big Raisin, oatmeal raisin cookies, Honeycrisp apples, clove, paprika, baseball glove.

PALATE: Honey Nut Cheerios, raisin-filled bread pudding with vanilla cream, roasted candied pecans (the kind you buy at baseball games), and leather; for as much flavor as there is here, the finish is pretty soft and dry.

RYE 100

I guess you could say the "100" is for both the proof and the 100% rye mash bill; made with Elbon Rye from Northwest Texas accompanied by crystal, chocolate, and roasted rye and pot distilled.

PROOF: 100

NOSE: Chai, toasted oak, fresh cracked pepper, chocolate milk with FAR too much Hershey's in it, cherries.

PALATE: Butterscotch pudding, warm habanero spiced mocha, make that warm habanero spiced mocha with 2 shots of espresso, finishes with a little bit of a Reese's Peanut Butter Cup vibe.

TEXAS RYE CASK STRENGTH

This is a cask strength version of the Rye 100 that is 30 months old, which is twice as old as its little brother.

PROOF: 125

NOSE: Waffle cone, caramelized pecan crumble, cinnamon, slight fennel.

PALATE: When you threw the bell peppers on the grill but forgot about them, hot and spicy, long finish that moves the spice from your tongue to the back of your throat and back, caramelized onion, ginger snaps, campfire.

MIRADOR

Mirador is a blend of whiskies ranging from under 2 years to almost 5 years in age but because all of the aging took place in used casks it's quite soft for a Balcones expression.

PROOF: 109.6

NOSE: Fresh pear and green apple, over-ripe pear and green apples, honeysuckle, the first day of fall, brown sugar and soft suede leather.

PALATE: Green tea with honey, mussels in a lemongrass-fennel sauce, apple pie with lemon curd, fruit salad with marshmallows and pecans, citrus twang, hint of a marmalade finish before ending with Earl Grey tea.

HIGH PLAINS

Using barley developed at Texas A&M, this was a collaboration with Blacklands Malt and is 100% Texas grain.

PROOF: 114

NOSE: Lemonheads, demerara sugar, whipped cream, tomato sauce being cooked but before you add the garlic.

PALATE: Green bean casserole, fried onions, full bodied, Frank's Red Hot Sauce, Squirt soda, ethanol, citrus pith, and my wife's tasting note is "Whoa, that's hot, whoa."

WHEATED BOURBON

Introduced for their 10th anniversary, this is made from a mash of blue corn, Texas red winter wheat, and Golden Promise barley.

PROOF: 122

NOSE: A new pack of Big League Chew (does that still exist?), vanilla pudding, Old English wood polish

PALATE: Oily, burnt sugar caramel pie, cowboy boots, Pecan Sandies

LINEAGE TEXAS SINGLE MALT

This is made using a combination of Scottish-grown Golden Promise as well as malted barley grown in the Texas High Plains and aged in both refill and new oak barrels. The idea behind Lineage was to create the "most accessible Single Malt yet in both taste profile and price."

PROOF: 94

NOSE: Sweet vanilla cream, brown gravy, hot spiced cider, over ripe bananas, stone fruit.

PALATE: Dulce de leche, Manuka honey, sweet potato, Malbec, late palate black tea and cinnamon, cigarette tobacco also lingers.

18-163

BATCH: BWW
PROOF: 122.7

BANNER DISTILLING Cº

DSP-TX-20012

FILL DATE: 11/25/18
DUMP DATE:
EMPTY WT: 37.8
FULL WT: 125.6

BANNER DISTILLING

DRIVING UP TO BANNER DISTILLING feels like the beginning of a Zac Efron rom-com about a plucky young distiller who's just trying to realize his dream. The road is paved, mostly, and the distillery sits in the middle of a sea of corn and wheat. As you walk past the water tower and into the barn-turned-tasting room, you get the immediate sense that everything you see has been fought for.

In 2011, Logan Simpson and Tony Jimenez came together because of a passion for craft beer, but it was the discovery of a mutual love of whiskey that led them to create Banner. They are the ultimate DIY distilling story. They literally googled their way into building a small still on $300, using parts from a plumbing supply company and a beer keg they bought off Craigslist, although I'm sure Simpson's doctorate in chemistry and Jimenez's equipment engineering background helped.

Banner is tiny. Those who have had Banner are in a very, very small club. To date, they producedw made less than 1,500 bottles of their flagship Banner Wheat Whiskey made with locally-sourced wheat. And when I say "locally-sourced," I mean that when they began, the wheat was legitimately grown next door. If "estate" whiskey was a category, Banner would be on the list. Also, their micro-batches are proofed down using rainwater. They're as grain to glass as you can get.

Banner Wheat Whiskey took home a Silver at the New York International Spirits Competition and a Gold in the granddaddy of them all, the San Francisco World Spirits Competition. Banner Wheat Whiskey is truly made from Texas, and made for Texas.

BANNER WHEAT WHISKEY

100% local grain to glass, made with rainwater, 95% winter wheat, 5% Texas malted barley, which makes it soft on the palate; only available in 375ml bottles.

 PROOF: 92

 NOSE: Sugar-soaked cherries, burnt caramel sauce, sweet wheat.

 PALATE: Whole-grain bread, horchata, peppery, and chocolate-covered cherry finish.

BANNER®

Texas original!

Wheat
WHISKEY

SMALL BATCH  MILL-TO-STILL
WITH TEXAS RAIN & GRAIN

TEXAS MADE

375 ML
46% ALC/VOL

Handcrafted | MANOR, TX
Distilled & bottled by **Banner Distilling Co.**

COME AND TAK
BANNER DISTILLING CO
BANNE
VODKA
BANNER DISTILLI
BANN
WHISK
TEXAS MA
BA
DISTILLI
Columbia
DIST

KOOPER FAMILY WHISKEY COMPANY

ON THE HIGHWAY THAT RUNS BETWEEN Austin and Houston, there's a sleepy little town called Ledbetter, population 860. There's also the best little blending house in Texas: Kooper Family Whiskey Company. They are 100% family owned and operated by Michelle and Troy Kooper, who both left corporate jobs and founded their blending house in 2012.

When you pull up to Kooper Family, it feels like you've found a magical speakeasy in a ghost town. Outside of the tasting room doors is an unincorporated town, split by a major highway. But inside, it's classy and romantic. The barn-style tasting room doubles as their rickhouse and is lined with barrels of whiskey and there's a record playing old Elvis love ballads. You'll also find a serenity only possible in a small Texas town.

It feels like it's somehow nicer than it should be, but not in a bad way. "You know, it's pretty shabby looking, but you come inside and you're wowed," said Troy. "Imagine this in Austin. You'd expect it to be nice, but the surprise and delight that people get walking in here is great." And delight is certainly something that Kooper Family does.

In 2015, Kooper Family bought 175 gallons of unaged rye whiskey from Koval Distillery in Chicago, threw it into barrels, and brought it home to Texas to begin aging. This was released as Kooper Family 100% Rye Whiskey. More importantly, this became the base of the idea to become a blending house. In fact, the decision to move from the Hill Country to Ledbetter was partially in search of a balance of humidity, and being situated between the humidity of the Gulf Coast and the dry heat of the Hill Country wound up being exactly what the Koopers were seeking.

Currently, Kooper Family is working with distillates from Kentucky, Indiana, Tennessee, and Illinois, with all sorts of different ages. Kooper Family also uses a variety of barrels, from new American oak to toasted French oak to reusing various wine and spirits barrels.

Everything about Kooper Family, from the vibe of their tasting room to the image of their grandfather, Howard, on their Kooper Family Rye, is rooted in family. "You know it's just Michelle and I. We don't have any employees," said Troy. "This is truly a labor of love. There's passion here. There's family here. And frankly, there's great whiskey here."

SWEETHEART OF THE RODEO

Distilled in Indiana from 75% corn, 21% rye, and 4% barley, barreled in new #3 char new American white oak casks, and aged in Texas for at least 4 years.

PROOF: 90

NOSE: Savory, green tobacco leaves, toasted walnuts, orange marmalade.

PALATE: Honeycomb, warm mulling spices, almond toffee popcorn, sweet finish.

KOOPER FAMILY RYE

95% rye from MGP, aged for at least 3 years and with 51% rye from Tennessee, aged for at least 5 years, blended then re-barreled in bourbon barrels.

PROOF: 90

NOSE: Dill, the burnt part of crème brûlée, raisins and figs.

PALATE: Cinnamon bark, melted butter, vanilla syrup (the kind you'd put in your coffee), baking spices.

PRODIGAL SON BOURBON

Slowly matured Kentucky sour mash, aged in Texas; 78% corn, 10% rye, 12% malt, only 5 barrels made and sold exclusively in the Kooper Family tasting room.

PROOF: 86

NOSE: Vanilla extract, lemon zest, buttered pound cake.

PALATE: Subtle spice and cream notes, toffee accents, burnt sugar, Atomic Fireball finish.

OAK & EDEN

WHISKEY IS INHERENTLY STEEPED IN TRADITION. This makes it very, very easy for people to only believe what they've been told about certain whiskeys and/or to develop strong opinions about those who make whiskey but do not abide by the established traditions. It's become so incredibly easy for whiskey lovers to discount innovation that when a company comes out with something that could truly change the way that whiskey is approached, they are immediately seen as suspect. How dare they?

My favorite thing about Texas whiskey, specifically, is that we don't have those traditions. Creativity is the name of the game here, which is why it makes perfect sense that a brand like Oak & Eden started in this wild west whiskey industry we're building. Brothers Joe and Jamie Giildenzopf, along with Brad Neathery, created Oak & Eden as a way to do their best to individualize the whiskey. They have patented a process they are calling "in-bottle finishing," which involves adding a wooden "spire" that allows them to create different finishes on a per bottle level. Nothing like this has ever been done.

Finished whiskey is nothing new. While started by Scotch makers, finishing as a way to accent or enhance flavors has been used with all sorts of spirits, but the common thread has always been the use of a barrel. Port finishes, double barrels, I've seen High West Double Rye single barrel picks that have been finished in Barreled Manhattan barrels, but nothing has come close to this approach. When Maker's Mark released their Maker's 46, they used various types of barrel staves at various char levels as a fantastic way to impact the flavor profile of that whiskey. But that was still by the barrel. Oak & Eden works on a micro-level.

If you've been around whiskey for a bit, you've no doubt seen those oak infusion spirals that allow you to "age" your own whiskey. I'm not going to tell you that they aren't effective in creating the illusion of aging, but I'll certainly tell you that the illusion is mediocre at best. So when presented with an Oak & Eden bottle that has a spiraled piece of wood inside, remember the intention. "The goal of the spire is to impart more flavor to the whiskey by finishing it, not as a substitute for additional aging," said Joe. Every bottle of Oak & Eden contains a 5-inch long spiral-cut piece of wood, but each of those spires is created to specifically impart different finishes. "The impact of the spire is exhausted after six weeks," Joe told me.

Unapologetically, all of their whiskies are sourced, mostly from MGP, and they do not age their whiskey in Texas, as they believe that the environment is a little extreme for their purposes. All of their whiskey is three years old. Oak & Eden has won Double Gold at San Francisco World Spirits Competition and the International Wine & Spirits Festival and countless number of golds at a variety of spirits competitions.

"I had just sold my company and my brother Jamie sent me a jar of home-distilled whiskey he had put a stave in as a congratulations," Joe told me. "I say stave. It was actually just a chunk of wood from a barrel. He was so proud of it. So I called him and I know he was so proud of it and just waiting for me to say how much I liked it. But instead I said, 'Tell me about this wood in the jar. Has anyone done that before?' He said no, I said why? And he said that would be stupid. So I spent the next nine months investigating the market to see if this was something we should do."

The other thing that is very interesting about Oak & Eden is their plan to create tasting rooms across the state of Texas where they will allow consumers to, eventually, create their own bottle's individual profile. You will literally be able to order a single bottle to your specifications. Not only is this one of the most clever and innovative approaches to whiskey, but it's tasty as hell. Look for the Nico Martini Cask Strength, Madeira Spire Finished, Wheated Rye version of Oak & Eden... okay, not really. But, I guess you never know.

WHEAT AND SPIRE

A sourced wheated bourbon, which is 51% corn, 45% wheat, and 5% malted barley, then bottled with a medium charred, then lightly toasted French oak spire.

PROOF: 90

NOSE: Vanilla, cherry tart, butterscotch, whole wheat bagels.

PALATE: Mixed berry jam, the pricey maraschino cherries from the jar, roasted marshmallow just before it catches on fire.

RYE AND SPIRE

A sourced rye whiskey, which is 95% rye and 5% malted barley, then bottled with a heavy charred American oak spire

PROOF: 90

NOSE: Cinnamon and clove, ground ginger, the hand-rolled cigar station at the last whiskey festival you went to.

PALATE: The dark part of a cinnamon roll, licorice, slight cigar box vibe, salted caramel mudslide.

RYE WITH
RAHR & SONS BREWING

The same Oak & Eden Rye bottled with a lightly toasted American oak spire that has been soaked in Rahr & Sons Brewing Dadgum IPA.

PROOF: 90

NOSE: Canned pineapple, hint of cedar, hot milk with cinnamon.

PALATE: Hoppy but not overpoweringly, fennel, gingerbread, slightly lemony in a piney way.

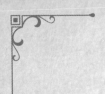

RIO BRAZOS DISTILLERY

If you're not from Texas and you're reading this, know this: Aggies (those who have attended the University of Texas A&M) are some of the most loyal of all Texans. Just ask them. Even though I'm a diehard Texas Longhorns fan, I'll certainly give them that. They're usually crazy, but I digress...

Nathan Barkman, the owner and operator of the Rio Brazos Distillery, knows all about that Aggie loyalty. It's the thing that's been driving his operation for years, but how he got into this game is a bit of a saga. "I was in Alaska as the managing editor of a newspaper out there, living in a woodshed out on the tundra and my now wife came out to visit me. While she was there the shed burned down. We literally lost everything that we owned and there's not a lot of options as far as where to live, so we wound up staying in the attic of this Vietnam vet. He taught me how to retread my snowmobile, how to drift net for salmon, and, most importantly, he taught me how to use a soldering iron, a 55-gallon drum, and a copper coil to turn cornmeal and flour into whiskey," Barkman told me. When he moved back down south, he and his brother Wade started Republic 1836 Steakhouse, and he started to get back into home brewing. In 2012, he sold his portion of the steakhouse and launched the hometown distillery for Bryan-College Station in 2013.

Rio Brazo Distillery is 100% Texas grain to glass even though, when he started, he couldn't get anyone to sell him non-GMO corn. Now, he's dedicated and committed to making the most Texas product possible. Again, as a Texas fan who immediately finds all Aggies a little suspect, I asked him how his whiskey has been accepted by those in the area. "This is an incredible place to have a distillery. It's very much what you see is what you get and there has been some incredible support from them, even during the COVID nightmare. I have put so much sweat equity into this and it's amazing to be a part of this community that recognizes that."

TEXAS BOURBON WHISKEY

Twice distilled, 100% grain to glass, Texas corn, malted barley, soft winter wheat, double barreled: first in new American white oak for 9 months, then 9 months aged for an additional year in used bourbon barrels.

PROOF: 90

NOSE: Grilled mini red peppers, spice cake cookies, ground cinnamon.

PALATE: Vanilla bean pudding cake, hot buttered shortcake, toasted pistachio.

CHIMNEY HILL

A higher-proof version of the Texas Bourbon finished in a Sauternes cask; this single barrel selection is absolutely lovely and if you can find it, grab it.

PROOF: 110

NOSE: Ground ginger, chai tea, sawdust, cloves, vanilla custard.

PALATE: Oily, iced pound cake, black currant, pear-spiced cake.

SAINT LIBERTY WHISKEY

MARK SORELLE, THE FOUNDER OF SAINT LIBERTY WHISKEY, calls himself the company's chief historian. He had the idea for the brand as he read stories of Prohibition-era women bootleggers while researching brand concepts for his other job. "A lot of people don't realize that women were at the forefront of the liquor industry at one point," SoRelle said. The bottle is beautiful, the stories sound like miniature movies, or, at worst, a season three episode synopsis of *Boardwalk Empire*.

SoRelle had partnered with two distilleries for each whiskey released, and his Texas partner is Smithville's Bone Spirits. The first release, Bertie's Bear Gulch is a 4-year-old bourbon blend that is then sent to Montana's Lolo Creek Distillery, where it is proofed down using Montana water. Saint Liberty is one of those interesting brands that by virtue of being completely transparent in their presentation of the product helps spur the question "What is a Texas whiskey?" Are they discounted because they're proofing elsewhere? I'd say no, but I guess others may disagree.

Regardless of your allegiance, my favorite thing about Saint Liberty is the focus on the stories of some of the women who helped keep whiskey alive during Prohibition. Bertie Brown, the first whiskey's namesake, was known to make the best moonshine in Montana. She was killed in 1933, the year Prohibition ended, when her kitchen exploded. Additional products will lead to additional stories and additional ways to honor these women who have played an incredibly important role in American whiskey history.

MARY'S FOUR GRAIN

Sourced Central Texas 4-grain whiskey, proofed and bottled in Colorado with Rocky Mountain water; aged 4 years in a #3 char 53-gallon barrel with a mash bill of 65% local corn, 22% wheat, 10% rye, and 3% malted barley.

PROOF: 95

NOSE: Dried apricot, black tea, cinnamon, ginger snaps.

PALATE: Butterscotch syrup, caramel corn, Chinese five-spice, allspice up front and a creamy flan-like finish.

TEXAS WHISKEY FESTIVAL

Whiskey fans Jake and Michelle Clements and soon-to-be business partner Clayton Corn co-founded the Texas Whiskey Festival in 2017 after a conversation during SXSW found them naming all of their favorite Texas whiskeys. It was then and there that they realized there were, in fact, enough to warrant their own festival. The first Texas Whiskey Festival in 2018 hosted 500 people and eleven distilleries. The 2020 festival was on track to triple that attendance and the number of distilleries, but then COVID-19 hit.

The festival has multiple award categories, including a People's Choice category, which is voted on by dropping a wooden nickel in the basket of your favorite. Power to the people, and may the loudest team win. The other awards are selected by a panel of experts who judge in both bottled and grain-to-glass categories. It's amazing to see that even our consumer-facing festivals in this state are focused on transparency. "Many of the whiskeys mentioned [at that original SXSW chat] were misleading people through their label practices," Jake said. "There is nothing wrong with sourcing whiskey, just be truthful and if all you're doing is bottling in Texas, let consumers know."

For me, the most impressive element of the festival is the private bottled blends that have been created by partnering different distilleries each year in order to create a truly Texas blended whiskey, expertly blended by Daniel Whittington of Crowded Barrel. The first year's blend included Balcones, Ironroot, and Andalusia and the second year was Ranger Creek, Treaty Oak, and Lone Elm. Daniel then blends the spirits into one, truly, Texas whiskey and it's available for purchase at the festival, as well through Crowded Barrel (see page 294).

"These distillers have blazed the path creating an industry from scratch and aren't afraid to explore and push the boundaries. The creativity and willingness to experiment is what makes whiskey in Texas unique," said Jake. If you want the ultimate hack for tasting everything in this book, the Texas Whiskey Festival is it. I'll see you there?

SPIRIT OF TEXAS

THERE ARE VERY FEW DISTILLERIES in Texas that can celebrate a 10th anniversary. Spirit of Texas is one of the OG distilleries in the state and while they started with some incredible Texas pecan-enhanced rum, they've been selling their Pfluger Single Malt Whiskey since 2016. This gorgeous, light, and creamy spirit took gold at both the San Francisco World Spirits competition and the American Distilling Institute Competition, where they also won Best in Category.

The story is familiar: three friends, all of whom love to homebrew, have a few too many soda pops and decide to start a distillery. The difference here is that Shaun Siems, co-founder of Spirit of Texas, actually had the wherewithal to pull it off. His two original partners have since moved on, but Siems remains dedicated to making some of the best single malt whiskey in the state. "Getting into the distillery business, I definitely saw the single malt as the style I wanted to go with. I wanted to make a Scottish-style flavor profile that was very Texan, but in this style of whiskey that I love," said Siems.

The three founders, between them chemical, electrical, and mechanical engineers, were determined to build their own stills, Betsy and Bertha, from the ground up. The initial boiling pots were 150 and 180 gallon all-copper pots that were propane fired and paired with two 16" diameter columns with three plates on each column. "This created our triple-distilled process, which helps to make for an extra smooth distillation. Our columns are more of a hybrid style as we can remove the plates and go between a pot still and a column still setup," explained Siems. They have recently upgraded to 300-gallon boiling pots, as well as upgrading the size of the propane burners. Siems told me, "We have not named the new stills yet, but since they are identical we might just call them the Twins. Just like Texas BBQ, our secret to a perfect spirit is cooking it slow and low."

Spirit of Texas is a hometown distillery. They are Pflugerville through and through. The community has great pride in their home team, and you can feel the connection from the second you arrive. I've heard more people say "Spirit of Texas is my home distillery" than any other distillery in Texas. Spirit of Texas has done an amazing job of connecting to and serving its community. The fans will tell you that Spirit of Texas is as much a family as it is distillery.

PFLUGER
SINGLE MALT WHISKEY

This is 80% malted barley and 20% rye, three-times distilled and aged in new charred oak barrels. I lovingly call it "banana whiskey" and it's one of my favorite hidden gems.

PROOF: 92

NOSE: Banana bread, fresh apples, and almost an Orange Julius vibe.

PALATE: Mexican style flan, vanilla, nougat, baked peaches, smooth, and creamy mouthfeel.

STILL AUSTIN WHISKEY CO.

SMACK DAB IN THE MIDDLE of a business park in South Austin, you'll find Still Austin. This is the epitome of an urban distillery: it's modern, it's sleek, it's got a food truck, and a patio to hang out on with your dog. As you walk up, you pass a beautiful mural on the side wall before you're ushered into a gorgeous tasting room that feels like you're in a gallery that, thankfully, has a massive bar in it. Most importantly, this place feels like Austin.

The glaringly apparent attention to detail at Still Austin is entrenched in their desire to be all things Austin. "We put a high value on the growers in our region. Making something that's incredibly high quality was our first commitment," said founder Chris Seals. "From the very beginning, we wanted to showcase the grains that grow in our region and have a unique flavor profile that kind of gives you a sense of who we are as people. We have never sourced any grains from outside Texas.

"We are committed to be as sustainable as possible. The way that we operate with zero waste and with the way that we do our purchasing, not only are we able to keep more money in the pockets of our neighbors, but when you think about how to reduce your carbon footprint, you want to be as local as possible. I'm very proud to say that we were invited by the EPA to be part of the creation of the Energy Star certification for distilleries. Instead of using yellow dent corn like a large amount of whiskey makers, we use white corn, the kind you make tortillas out of. We also use red winter wheat that's grown in Travis County, and barley that's grown in Brady, Texas." This is truly central Texas in a glass.

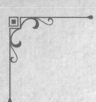
One thing that truly grabbed my attention was when Seals told me their master blender was Nancy Fraley. Fraley is one of the most respected and sought after whiskey whisperers in the world. Having worked with a dozen incredible brands that you no doubt know, and countless others who we may or may not be able to talk about it, Fraley has been advising on barrel selection, aging times, and creating a legacy of innovation with her blending methodology for years.

One of the most important techniques that Fraley encourages is élevage. This French technique most commonly applied to making Cognac and Armagnac is an all-encompassing approach to barrels, individually caring for each one of them. Head distiller John Schrepel said, "Once or twice a month, we unstack and open every barrel, to test the proof and add water to proof it down in the barrel. It's a ton of effort, but the impact on the whiskey itself is amazing." This particular process is a "slow reduction," and it is used to help to maintain the gentle oak aromas and to create a distinct mouthfeel that is softer with more finesse and complexity. Still Austin's whiskeys are much less aggressive than the majority of Texas whiskeys and these techniques are creating very grain-forward expressions that are incredibly flavorful.

In August 2020, Still Austin released their flagship straight bourbon whiskey. The label on the bottle is a commissioned artwork by native Texan Marc Burckhardt, and most of Still Austin's upcoming releases will be a series of portraits of "archetypical" Austinites. This label is called "the Musician," and future labels will feature archetypal figures like the Naturalist, the Writer, the Visionary, and the Artist. With Austin being "The Live Music Capital of the World," this is the perfect start to the series. It's easily the most beautiful bottle in the state.

THE MUSICIAN STRAIGHT BOURBON WHISKEY

Entirely grain to glass, which will be true of everything this distillery turns out; the mash bill is 70% white corn, 25% Elbon rye, 5% Wildfire malted barley, aged for at least 2 years.

 PROOF: 98.4

 NOSE: Charred bananas, hazelnut, orange zest, grilled pears.

 PALATE: Ground cinnamon, caramel apple crumble, rice pudding, finishing with never-ending black pepper and maraschino cherries.

STILL AUSTIN

THE MUSICIAN

STRAIGHT BOURBON WHISKEY

— 49.2% ALC/VOL | 98.4 PROOF —

STILL AUSTIN

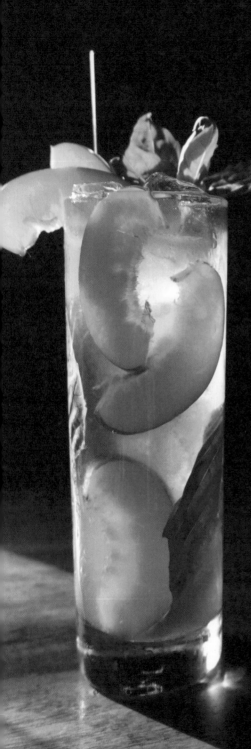

QUIET LIGHT

Rosey Sullivan, founder of the all-female cocktail competition The Shake Up, tends bar at Armoury DE in the Deep Ellum neighborhood of Dallas. This light and refreshing cocktail created by Sullivan gets its sweet tang from the Nectarine Shrub, made with champagne vinegar. Allowing the fruit to marinate in sugar for two days draws out its full flavor, which complements the whiskey's ripe aroma of tropical fruit and rye spice.

2 oz. Still Austin Straight Bourbon Whiskey

1½ oz. Nectarine Shrub

3–4 basil leaves

Topo Chico

1. Combine the whiskey, shrub and basil leaves in a highball. Stir for 20 seconds. Fill the glass with ice, give it a few more stirs then top with Topo Chico. Garnish with a sprig of basil and a few slices of nectarine.

Nectarine Shrub: Add 1 cup mashed ripe nectarines to a bowl and top with 1 cup sugar. Cover the bowl and refrigerate for 2 days. Add 1 cup champagne vinegar, stir well, and let the mixture sit for 10 minutes before straining. Store in refrigerator for up to 6 months.

STARTING A TEXAS DISTILLERY

CHRIS SEALS

When I was growing up, the one bit of advice I probably heard from my dad more than any other was an admonition not to take a short-cut or do a half-hearted job. My dad's phrase—which he said exactly the same way each time and with a tone that reminded me that he had said it a thousand times before—was: "Anything worth doing is worth doing right." It's the sort of phrase I heard so much that I could hear him say it before he said it. It was his way of saying that, when you do the right thing, it isn't going to be painless. This was my dad's gentle way of instilling in his sons and daughter a focus on excellence, a pride and satisfaction in a hard-earned achievement, and a determination to go far beyond the minimum required. Doing it the right way. That phrase has been used to describe how we do things at Still Austin Whiskey, with a dedication to excellence.

As I write this note in September 2020, we are now more than seven years past the day my dad came to me and asked me to join him in building an artisan whiskey distillery. And we are just six weeks past the day we released our first straight bourbon, the Musician. We have gone very slowly. From the day we first visited with Austin city officials about the novel ideal of building a craft whiskey distillery in the heart of our city, till the day they finally approved the project, the process took thirty-seven months. Add to that a year of prior dreaming and planning, and years of perfecting our technique. Why did it take us seven years to release this expression—and why would we do this in the first place?

A big part of our vision was the wish to create a genuine expression of Austin. While Texas as a state is known for independence, hard work, and pride (everything is bigger in Texas, right?), the mythology of the heart of Texas—Austin—is unique. We value what makes us different (after all, "Keep Austin Weird" is the unofficial slogan of city), and we are known for our creativity, our freewheeling lifestyle, and live music. Since we wanted to make a spirit that is genuinely "of Austin," we started with the grain. One hundred percent of our grains is grown locally by Texas farmers. This is more difficult to do than it sounds and to my knowledge we are the first (and perhaps only?) distillery in Texas where all of everything we have ever made is made from grains grown on a Texas farm. We also use grain varieties that are part of our local culture, like the white corn that you'll also find in Austin's Tex-Mex corn chips and corn tortillas, and Texas-grown rye, which is both sweet and spicy. Growing grains requires an intuitive awareness of the changing seasons. And working with farmers to source all of them here, in our state, takes years of planning.

We wanted to bring out the flavor of our local grain. At the outset we imagined doing that on the kind of pot stills we saw popping up at craft distilleries across the US. But then we met Michael Delevante, a master distiller who today has 59 years of experience distilling at some of the most innovative and respected distilleries in the world. Mike challenged our preconceived notions. He told us that if we truly wanted to bring out the delicious flavors of our local grains, we would have to construct "the best craft distillery that's ever been built." That phrase alone led us to hire Mike as our distillery designer. He challenged us to construct a one-of-a-kind craft column still, one different from any he had built in his very long career of still design. This idea shocked and puzzled us. In our studies of stills, we'd come to view the column still as a sort of less-specialized, high-volume production machine. But Mike convinced us that, if we were to design our column still the right way, it would give us unparalleled control over the quality of the spirit. His design, which includes twelve rectifying trays—compare that to the three or four typically found on most column stills—helped us to isolate and bring out the flavors from our local grains. In fact, those flavors have helped to give our bourbon a flavor that is distinct from anything bourbon lovers have ever tasted.

To construct our 42-foot craft column still we called upon Forsyths of Scotland, the most experienced still-maker in the world. It took a long time to design her, bring her from Scotland, and install her, but the extra time and effort were worth it for the quality of spirit she makes today. Once she was completed, we lovingly named her Nancy (after the lead character in the film *Attack of the 50-Foot Woman*). At the time of this writing she remains the only Forsyths craft column still in America, as unusual and unique as the city she calls home.

With the help of another Nancy on our team—legendary master blender Nancy Fraley—we fill and mature our barrels using the unique and ancient French technique of slow-water reduction (or, as some have called it, "slow cut"). The process is extra labor intensive and involves slowly reducing the spirit while it's in the barrel by adding water a little at a time over a period of years. This process is perfectly suited to the Central Texas climate, giving us the control to fine-tune each barrel and raise it to the highest quality. This meticulous process slows down the maturation of the spirit; by taking more time, we create something that we're quite proud to call our own.

Over the past year, this process caused our barrels to mature with a flavor all its own—a flavor we love. To celebrate, we hired a world-renowned local artist, Marc Burkhardt, to paint a series of portraits of who we are as Austinites. This series is what we call a "New Mythology" of Austin, showing the kind of people we are, the people who've made us us, and the people we aspire to be. Marc's portrait of the Musician honors the musicians of our state, especially those who sing in the Live Music Capital of the World. In Marc's painting, I can hear the softness, gentleness, and finesse of the Musician's voice. This is the spirit in the bourbon we've made—and most importantly, these are qualities I see in my own daughters. They are strong and unafraid. They are prepared to rise up and attain every dream they have. They are truly unique, with beauty that defies description. And they carry within them a little of me—and a little of my dad.

Ask anyone at Still Austin Whiskey Co. what they love most about us, and I think you'll hear some version of the same thing: "The quality"; "We never cut a corner"; "We always do things the right way." Doing our best is never going to be fast or easy. But doing our best makes us who we are: an expression of the city we love, offering optimism for a future populated by our best selves.

Chris Seals is the founder of Still Austin Whiskey Co.

HILL COUNTRY AND SOUTH TEXAS ★

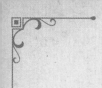

Hill Country and South Texas

FOR THOSE OF YOU WHO HAVE DECIDED to use this book to plan your ultimate Texas whiskey adventure, this is the section you were looking for. There's something so unique about the Texas Hill Country and something every visitor to the great state should experience. In the mid-19th century, this area was primarily settled by German, Swiss, Austrian, and Czech immigrants. In concert with some of the most beautiful scenery in the state, these Old World European roots created a microculture within Texas. Most importantly, this is our Napa Valley. Texas wine has become increasingly impressive and this is easily one of the most tourist-friendly areas in the state. It's also producing some of the best whiskey anywhere. In Austin or San Antonio for a day and want to make it out? Head to Blanco. The Blanco Hat Trick covers Andalusia, Milam & Greene, and Real Spirits and is a fantastic way to experience three completely different types of whiskey.

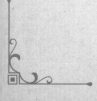

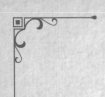

ANDALUSIA WHISKEY COMPANY

WHILE BRAINSTORMING POSSIBLE NAMES for their distillery, Tommy Erwin and Ty Phelps came across some old papers that showed that Phelps's family land, where they were building their distillery, was once called Andalusia Ranches. Erwin and his wife lived in Spain for a while and the area reminded them of that country's Andalucia region, so they thought the Andalusia Whiskey Company was perfect.

Erwin and Phelps met while both of them were working at Real Ale in Blanco, just down the road from their current distillery. Erwin was the microbiologist running the lab and Phelps was the head brewer. After repeated conversations about combining their powers, Andalusia Whiskey Company was born to be a family venture. They built the entire tasting room by hand, with both of their families chipping in.

The production facility is zero waste. They feed their spent grain to the sheep, cattle, llama, Dolly (Dolly Llama, get it?), and chickens that surround the distillery. When they realized that the water on the property wasn't what they were looking for, they decided to put in a 56,000-gallon rainwater collection tank system to help conserve as much water as possible. Their whiskey is made entirely from rainwater, which they use for literally everything at their facility. Andalusia is, without question, one of the most stubborn of all Texas distilleries when it comes to being true to their state and their terroir. They are fully grain to glass, from the ground up, and have never sourced anything. Every drop coming out of Andalusia is a Texas Certified Whiskey (see page 40).

"I am not a bourbon guy. It's just not my thing," Phelps told me. In fact, I was visiting Crowded Barrel right before heading down to Blanco and I mentioned it to Daniel Whittington, to which he replied, "Oh man, yeah, Ty hates bourbon.

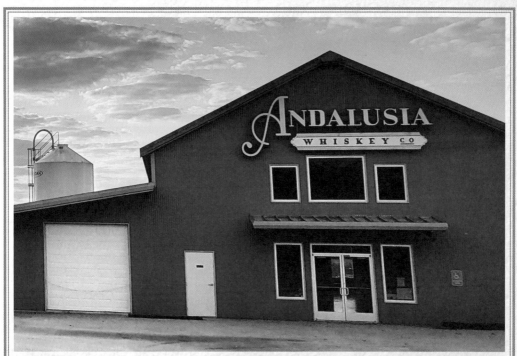

He'll probably deny it, but man, he hates bourbon." Thankfully, this is Texas and we're not really interested in being forced into any particular kind of whiskey, like other, more volume-producing states with lots of Es and Ks in their names. "I spent several years thinking I wasn't a whiskey guy, but I just had to find my niche. I'm not a bourbon guy. Not my thing," Phelps admitted with a laugh. "It was a few craft distilleries in the US like Stranahan's and Westland that introduced me to American, non-peated single malts. They're also ex-brewers and they were using specialty malts to create different flavors, which was not something commonly done in the whiskey industry." You could use a chocolate malt to pull out deep chocolate flavors or you could use a crystal malt for a honey biscuit note, for example. It's incredible that more distillers don't utilize malt varieties in their whiskey making and those who truly believe it doesn't matter don't have enough sense to spit downwind.

"I had been a craft brewer by trade for most of my life. It was a pretty easy transition into distilling, especially malt whiskey. We had a good portion of the process down, but obviously I had to learn the distilling part of it. But it's definitely a close cousin to brewing," said Phelps. "We take much more of a brewer's approach to our malts. We've used klin malts, caramel malts, roasted malts, and we roast malts."

Andalusia, as of now, is 100% malted barley. They have built their distillery specifically to handle whiskey in this manner. Their focus is creating very Texan whiskeys but they honor the style of the pot still distillations from Ireland and Scotland. Phelps said, "We are literally just trying to make something great and hoping that people like the same things that we like." We do, brother, we do.

Andalusia peat smokes their own grain, which is another testament to Andalusia's dedication to their craft. There are only a handful of distilleries outside of Scotland that are doing peated whiskeys but they mostly order peated malt from there. "The construction of our smokehouse allowed us to have more options once we were able to source some peat and smoke our own. It's been awesome to be able to vary the types of peat, levels of peat, and smoking duration. Peat's tough to find. We're literally buying from Amazon because this consumer facing product came out for Irish folks around the world who used to smoke peat in their fireplaces." Phelp uses a process of wetting the grain before smoking it in order for the barley to make it a little more sticky so that it grabs on to the peat a lot more than otherwise. They smoke the grain for about twenty-four hours in

their custom-built smokehouse. As with most of the conversations about smoking things in Texas, low and slow is the best way to smoke. And then, of course, once you have the smokehouse built, you can experiment with other woods to smoke grain, which leads you to create a product like their Stryker, made of grain that has been smoked in the more traditional Texas barbecue style of oak, mesquite, and applewood.

The distillery is completely hands-on. If you visit, Phelps will show you whatever you want to see. He may talk you into helping bottle in exchange for some access, but you'll see anything and everything you could imagine about his process. There are no secrets here and you couldn't find a falsehood if you tried.

"For the last four years, we've been head down, just focused on the whiskey. Our marketing budget last year was about $100 that we spent on Facebook ads. We just needed to invest every penny that we had on grain and malt," Phelps said. "It's actually been great recently because all of the fun projects that we put down two or three years ago are starting to be ready. We're always trying new and fun projects, but they're a few years away and it can be frustrating and a little scary. You don't get to really try anything or even know if it was a good idea."

"I think the biggest thing that makes a Texas whiskey unique is the aging environment," Phelps also told me. "There's definitely a lot of things like creativity and not feeling the need to stick to the tradition of older American whiskey regions, but I feel that the thing that binds us together is the environment. Our whiskey is different because of the climate." The climate of Texas is everything. That's the biggest thing that sticks out to me as I've been talking to all of these makers: the environment of Texas, not only from a climate standpoint, but from the culture that these craft makers operate within and the audiences that they create for. The environment of Texas is truly the key to the unique brand of whiskeys here. Andalusia might be our best example of what happens when you dial in on all of those elements with a laser focus.

Andalusia Whiskey is some of the best whiskey you'll find in America, let alone Texas. The care, effort, and creativity that is put into their whiskey is genuine. They believe that if they focus on making the best whiskey from the best grains, with the most sincere process, they will create a community that loves their whiskey. They don't need marketing. They just need you to taste the fruits of their labor. Ain't no slack in their rope.

BOTTLED-IN-BOND SINGLE MALT

The first Bottled-in-Bond whiskey in Texas; one of a kind and a beautifully round, even experience.

PROOF: 100

NOSE: Mounds candy bar, cherry compote, fresh-cut vanilla beans.

PALATE: Incredibly buttery, burnt hay, caramel flan, drinks hotter than its proof, red bell pepper, dandelion greens, expands dramatically mid-swallow, toasted oak.

TEXAS
SINGLE MALT

Grain-to-glass, triple-distilled single malt whiskey: "This meets all qualifications of an Irish whiskey. If it was made in Ireland, it would be considered a traditional Irish whiskey." This is a smoother, lighter whiskey that's all about the brightness of the barley.

 PROOF: 100

 NOSE: Vanilla bean souffle, waffle cone, orange blossom honey.

 PALATE: Fresh coconut oil, vanilla-iced sugar cookies, the top part of an apple crumble, salted caramel bars, toasted oak.

REVENANT OAK

This peated single malt whiskey is grain to glass and aged in used bourbon barrels; double-distilled with American malt, peated on property, this is a nod to classic Scotch whisky.

PROOF: 100

NOSE: Light-medium peat, vanilla, crème brulee, the custard inside of an éclair.

PALATE: Sweet and nuanced, cereal-like, earthy, newly lit cigar, buttermilk pecan pralines, a hint of peat smoke that finishes with a sweet little kiss before strutting out the door.

STRYKER

Grain-to-glass single malt whiskey smoked in the tradition of Texas BBQ with oak, mesquite, and applewood; aged in new charred barrels.

PROOF: 100

NOSE: Smoked beef ribs, campfire, Mexican vanilla extract.

PALATE: Overwhelmingly meaty, warm, leather, dark chocolate, candied burnt ends, mouth-coating and long on the finish.

RAINWATER

TY PHELPS

Water of Life: it translates as *aqua vitae* in Latin, or *uisge beatha* in Scottish Gaelic. Even if ancient distillers did not fully understand every step of their practice, they knew that water was an essential ingredient and the vehicle for alcohol and the other flavor compounds mysteriously produced during fermentation. They also discovered that altering the source and quality of water could dramatically impact the final distilled spirit.

Water hardness, alkalinity, and pH are determined by the amount of minerals and dissolved salts present in water. Hard water contains larger amounts of calcium and magnesium in solution, while soft water contains little to none. These characteristics play a large part in whiskey production. During the mashing process, calcium buffers the alkalinity of malt and helps create an ideal pH for enzyme conversion of starch to sugar. Other trace minerals such as zinc are important to maintain yeast health during fermentation.

Traditionally, beer breweries and whiskey distilleries were located in areas that were known to have a certain type or quality of water. Beer and whiskey styles have evolved based on the characteristics of local water sources. Pilsners were developed using the soft water found in Czechoslovakia. British ales flowed from the hard water of the Burton upon Trent (famous for high levels of gypsum.) The limestone water of Kentucky was found to be ideal for cooking corn and proofing bourbon.

Today, water chemistry is more widely understood. Production sites are no longer chosen for local water qualities, namely because pH can be adjusted using lactic, phosphoric, or citric acids. Hardness and alkalinity can be adjusted with the addition of calcium compounds. A distiller can now make a wide variety of products with a single source by changing the chemistry of the water for each specific product.

When scouting a location for Andalusia Whiskey in 2015, we chose our family's 117-acre cattle and sheep ranch about six miles north of Blanco. It offered sweeping Hill Country views and plenty of room to build and eventually expand.

Located on a major US highway, power lines were close-by and easily accessible, but soon a major problem arose: the farm's well water was very hard. It had extremely high levels of calcium and iron. Iron in proofing water can make whiskey turn black, which was not exactly an appealing prospect. Ever had whiskey turn black in a cheap flask? That's likely iron.

Our solution was to erect a 56,000-gallon water tank and collect every drop of rain that fell on the metal roof of the distillery building. While ours is not the first distillery to use rainwater during the production of whiskey, we are one of the few distilleries that rely on it for all of our water needs. Rainwater is essentially distilled water and can be thought of as a blank canvas—ready to dissolve minerals into solution that will give the water a particular character. Rainwater is ideal for nearly every step of the whiskey making process except one: mash water. For mashing water, we can add calcium in the form of calcium chloride or calcium sulfate (gypsum) in order to dial in the water hardness and alkalinity to a suitable level. Finally, before use the rainwater is also sediment filtered, carbon filtered, and UV light sterilized.

For every one inch of rainfall, the distillery's water tank collects 3,700 gallons of rainwater. The average local annual rainfall of thirty inches is enough to fill the tank twice over. Most families have enough rain falling on their roofs at home to supply themselves year-round. The challenge becomes having a tank large enough to save the water that falls in the rainy months to last throughout the dry summer months.

Over 90,000 bottles and five years later, the distillery has been fortunate to have never run out of rainwater. So pray for rain, because that next drop of rain might find its way into your whiskey glass!

Ty Phelps is the co-founder of Andalusia Whiskey Company.

CROWDED BARREL
WHISKEY COMPANY

Put your money where your mouth is. The entire concept of that statement is one of the most Texan ideals that I can think of. Crowded Barrel Whiskey Company is the final step in a long series of fortunate events, culminating in a couple of fellas throwing down a gauntlet and proving that what they teach is applicable. This, my friends, is the story of how those magnificent bastards started making whiskey.

Daniel Whittington got a call one day from his buddy Rex Williams. Rex's father Roy has been in corporate communications and advertising for decades, is a best-selling author, incredibly well respected in the industry, and in 2000 he started his school. The Wizard Academy is a non-traditional business school that focuses on new education techniques and is intentionally paradoxical. Their tag line is "We show you step-by-step how to do consciously what gifted people do unconsciously." Roy ran the program and the school for years but was looking for someone to take over as chancellor and he and Rex identified Daniel as the mark.

"Rex called me and said, 'My dad has a business school and he needs someone to run it so y'all should talk, then he told me it was called Wizard Academy. I immediately thought, whoa...I'm not doing that. That sounds like a cult," Daniel said. He wound up meeting Roy and loving the concept so much that he accepted. So there's the scene: our heroes, Daniel and Rex are a part of this magical land of wizardry, surrounded by Don Quixote paraphernalia, plopped in the middle of nowhere in Texas Hill Country, biding time before their next noble adventure.

A couple of years after taking over, Daniel constantly found himself hanging out with students after class and they would inevitably end up talking about whiskey. He found himself educating people as much in whiskey as he was in marketing. Daniel said, "I realized that there were amazing spirits training programs, but no one was teaching what we were teaching at the Wizard Academy in spirits specifically. No one was focusing on the communications and brain theory side of the industry. When I mentioned it to Roy he said 'let's do it,' and I said wait... Can we do that?" The Wizard Academy is an educational 501(c)3 and can technically teach whatever they want, so Roy told Daniel "We'll hold our first class in six months. Figure out what you're teaching and who you want to teach with and let's do it." The odyssey was about to be embarked upon.

The Whiskey Marketing School is like nothing else I've ever seen. In my past life I was pretty deep into digital marketing. I had (and still have) a small agency that I run, I was one of the first to receive an MA in Emerging Media and Communications from the University of Texas at Dallas, and I wound up teaching Digital Marketing Design and Branding Through Social Media for about four years at UTD. Braggart reel aside, I'm telling you this to lend credence to my level of understanding of "those" marketing schools and "those" marketing people. I've been to more tweet-ups and conferences based on meaningless, repetitive, self-aggrandizing, steamy piles of content than I'd like to admit. I know those guys. The Whiskey Marketing School is not that.

I've seen this method before, and I'll admit, it's a damn good one. The difference between the Whiskey Marketing School, the way that you'd expect a "whiskey school" to be taught is right there in the title. This is a program for those who are interested in becoming better at marketing whiskey. But naturally, the first step in any good marketing approach is knowing as much as you possibly can about the subject.

"We built it. We got people involved that we trusted and we built the concept. We wanted to teach the marketing and communications portion of the industry, but you have to teach the knowledge of whiskey... I mean it's awkward to have someone you're calling a whiskey sommelier not knowing that bourbon is 51% corn, but that was never the primary goal. I had no interest in opening a school based on a bunch of shit that you could just google," Daniel told me. "There are other schools doing an astounding job on the ins and outs of distillation. I didn't want to teach anyone how to run a still. What I wanted to teach people is what makes whiskey powerful, how to make money with a knowledge of whiskey, how to tell the story of whiskey, that kind of thing. The reason that we went with the word 'sommelier' was because that's what a good sommelier does. They make it a more human experience and take you on a journey. That's what we teach."

So as the days begin to grow longer and our heroes carried on in their state of vagabondage, a Haley's Comet of inspiration thundered down upon the beaten brow of Rex, rendering him helpless to the vision that a dramatic change was on the horizon. At that moment, he knew in his heart, he had no option other than a nemesis confrontation with the light of his life, his exalted partner, Daniel. Rex

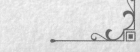

sashayed toward Daniel, cleared his throat in an obnoxious manner in order to gain the attention of his compatriot and said, "Hey man, you should start shooting YouTube videos."

"But I don't want to," countered Daniel.

"But, dude, you need to. We have all of this video equipment and editors on campus and, most importantly, you need to teach your sommeliers how to talk about whiskey in a non-snobby, non-assholey way," declared Rex.

"Okay. Fine," acquiesced Daniel.

The true calling of these magnificent bastards had been realized and they were on the precipice of greatness, overlooking a sea of opportunity and glory.

They started making videos and putting them online and after about a month, they exploded. All of a sudden, our heroes saw the path to their glorious future. They would use the internet to create a tribe of whiskey devotees. A tribe of people who didn't care to be snobby about whiskey. A sort of Whiskey Tribe, if you will. "Once it exploded, we both started to pay more attention. That's why Rex got interested. He said that he'd been trying to teach business owners about these subjects for years and he wanted to use the channel as a proving ground for the methods we were teaching," Daniel said.

It just kept growing and they started to get involved in the comments and the community exploded around them. "It felt like overnight, but it was probably about a year and we were the second whiskey channel to reach 100,000 subscribers on YouTube. The only reason we weren't the first was because we were about to beat Ralphy and we thought that was a bad look," Daniel told me. Ralfy hosts one of the OG YouTube whiskey shows. "Ralfy had been shooting videos for ten years. He's this adorable, grouchy old Scottish dude who's sort of seen as the Mr. Rodgers of whiskey YouTube. So, he'd been doing it for ten years and was at 96,000 subscribers and we had been doing it for a year and were at 98,000, because we knew what we're doing. And I was telling Rex that we had to do something because we were about to beat Ralfy, so we shot a video and told everyone to go subscribe to Ralfy to make sure he got there first and by his next video he was at 106,000. He did a response video but you could totally tell that he'd watched a couple of our videos and didn't really get it. We're just some weird mystery," Daniel said.

The Whiskey Tribe is polarizing, I guess. I've certainly seen people entirely discount them because they haven't "earned" it. I'm not sure if you've noticed, but there are some whiskey aficionados that are... how do you say... snobs. And some of the snobbiest of the snobby decide to start snobby whiskey blogs, create a podcast about their very, very serious approach to whiskey, or start highbrow YouTube review shows, declaring their opinions about whiskey so important that they must tell the world what they think. I put about as much stock in their opinions as I do the people who believe that if a whiskey isn't _____ from _____ then it couldn't possibly be good.

"One of the biggest reasons we have this reputation is that we didn't ask permission from anybody," Daniel said. "On the good side, there are a bunch of people who've spent thirty years in the industry and it just never occurred to them that you could do something like this and now that they've seen what we've done, they're now trying to share information and to teach people about whiskey in similar ways. It's amazing. But plenty of folks don't like us because we're new here and I get that. Then there are these others who've fashioned themselves as gatekeepers, and they spend their time trying to appear important. So when we started this and didn't ask any of them to be involved, quite a few of them got pretty butt-hurt about it. We are professional communicators. This is what we do, but when we'd mispronounce things because we didn't give a shit and make mistakes and dared to leave them in the video, they'd want us excommunicated. And when we'd dress up and have these insane storylines about demon battles between the Mooch and the Somm, forget about it. It's ridiculous. Some of them got really mad that we were winning."

So our heroes now have their tribe, but they need to figure out a way to make it all worthwhile. It was time, my friends, for monetization. The Whiskey Tribe on YouTube and Facebook is where you can find the insanity. The Whiskey Vault on YouTube is where you can find the whiskey specific educational content. They decided to split because, well frankly, while the Mooch and the Somm aren't everyone's cup of tea, the information in the vault is very straightforward and (mostly) informative. Part of the decision was also so that they could undo the nonprofit handcuffs and figure out a way to make some money with this time-suck because six videos a week is a massive amount of work. So the Tribe portion started a Patreon. Within one week, they were bringing in $15,000 a month.

"Shit! What are we going to do now?" asked Daniel.

"We can't take all that money every month and just say thanks guys!" lamented Rex.

"What a terrible look!" proclaimed Daniel.

MAN · MIKE GAYNOR · HECTOR MANUEL HERNANDEZ III · MATT STONE · MICHAEL HOUSER · KATIE SCHMALZ · BRIAN WICHART · CHRIS

MICHAEL CONNOLLY · DANIEL AMAYA · JOHN STUMP · MICHEAL ROZAR · CHRISTOPHER VELASQUEZ · CHRISTIAN GRIMES · CHRIS SM

O LOPEZ · MONTIE RYALS · JECK WHITE · MATT ROBERTS · MICHAEL IAGO · CHRIS KOMMER · BRYAN LUSHBOUGH · B

AXEL SON · NATHAN ADAMS · NICHOLAS DEROY · MICHAEL TOGUCHI · ROBERT EICHLER · ANDREW LEONARD · CHARLES

ELO WOLTERS · ERIN THOMPSON · MATT KIRK · ROBERT REECE · ROBERT SUMMERS · JAMES LEGIER · DAVIS HAHN · JASON

CHRISTOPHER HARGEFELDT · DANNY MORRIS · JESSE BIRMINGHAM · CURTIS TAKAHASHI · DAVID TÖCHTROP · DANIEL VENDET

ELTON BILLINGS · JEREMY TIEFEL · ANDRES MATA · DOUG GARRIS · CLAYTON YOUNG · FLORENCE EVENS · DARRYL

DAVID CARD · JEFFRY VAUGHAN · CHRISTOPHER ROTH · WYATT PAULEY · DALTON VAN PELT · JASON KUSZYNSKI

TIM WIDLUND · SCOTT THOMPSON · TRENT SUTTER · GABRIEL LOFQVIST · GIULIO LORETO · TODD COOPER

LOGAN DAVIS · GREG WILES · DAVE SHEPHERD · RON LIEBMAN · CODY PFEIL · TOM CRIMMINS · HEYDAD HELFER · SURRA

CK · GARRETT DUGGER · JORDAN ROBERTS · WILLIAM WINGFIELD · PATRICK LEE · TIM WILLIAMSON · PATRICK LARKIN

M SWATSKI · ISAAC GARCIA · GREGORY JISKRA · FREDRIK WELL-WATNE · JOEL KLANG · JOSEPH REGLIN · JORDAN FAY

PPE DESJARDINS · MIKE RYBCZYNSKI · JASON SHAY WERNER · PAT CODDINGTON · NATHAN WATROUS · PAUL DUERR

CK AHLUWALIA · PETER BENOIT · MICHAEL MORPHEW · PATRICK DREKER · NATHAN STANTON · JERED MAY · DAN MATLA

ADAM MCARTHUR · MURDOCH MACPHEE · ARLIE LONG · JASON STEELE · OCTAVIO MARTINEZ · NATHAN HEBERT · JAMES BALDWIN

S · PHILIP KRISTENSEN · NELSON HAMMER · PAUL MENDELSON · JACKSON BOLINGER · JEREMY FORSYTHE · PEDRO LOPEZ

ALDERAS · WILL DAVELAAR · JIMMY FARTHING · NICHOLAS MACREADY · MATTHEW ROSS · JASON ROSENBAUM · JS WELLS · DAV

MACK · NICHOLAS GODDARD · TREVOR DODGE · BENJAMIN NICELY · CHRISTOPHER JARMIN · JOHN GUENTZEL · DONOVAN YOUNG

TREVOR ROBENS · WILL BRENT · JOSHUA BARRTO · MITCHELL MARTIN · ERIC SOWDER · ZACHARY CLARK-WILLIAMS · JOSE

LEV SOLOMON · CHRIS WRIGHT · JOE D'ENTRONE · TONY CRONIN · MATTHEW PILGRIM · LEON D BACKER · DAV

GORY · TIMOTHY TODD · BRYAN HAARLSEN · SAM GALLIMORE · PANDORA REED · KOREY PETERSEN · JASON UNSWORTH · C

NOHN · COLUM LENNON · MICHAEL BAXTER · COREY WILLIS · PATRICK MINZE · RYAN LAYTON · RIC HASKEW · TY

RT DAVIDSON · RYAN JOHLE · WILLIAM SCHAPPERT · RUSSELL HUBBARD · BRIAN BRANSTEITTER · CHRIS JACINTO · DE

E · BEN STAHL · GODRICK HELLHAMMER · JAMES BALLOU · JAMES VINCENT RAP · JASON NEWMAN · BEN VALENCIA

GNIFICENCE

"If we had just taken the money, it would have only lasted like two months. You can't justify giving two asshats on YouTube 15K a month for content they were already going to make anyway. So we said, what if we start a distillery on the campus, which we had talked about doing anyway. I thought we could build a distillery, and make it legal, and it'll pay for itself because we could sell some drinks, and we'd have this resource. But when the Patreon blew up, we knew this was our opportunity to give the Tribe a mission," said Daniel.

Enter Crowded Barrel Whiskey Company. This is, by any metric I could find, the first crowdsourced whiskey company in history. The members of the Whiskey Tribe's Patreon decide everything about the company and what they make. They decided the name, the bottle shape and size, the corks, the grains, the yeasts, the proof, the barrel type, absolutely everything. Once they made that announcement, they sold out of their Patreon, which now brings in over $27,000 a week. They have remained sold out for the past two years. "We spend about $30,000 a quarter fulfilling our promises through the Patreon and 100% of it is funding the distillery and it's 100% the reason we're one of the few distilleries that aren't worried about going bankrupt during COVID, because unlike everyone else we have income like clockwork from this supportive fan base. We built it backward," Daniel told me.

The first decision the tribe made was on the type of distillery they were going to be. Start-up distillers have two ways to make money while they wait for whiskey to age. They can make young and unaged spirits like vodka or gin or white dog, or they can start sourcing older whiskey from other distilleries. They all voted on sourcing, they voted on MGP, they voted on the mash bill, and Crowded Barrel bought twelve barrels to bring back home. "We sat on them for about a year and the Texas heat really affected them, so they voted on releasing them one barrel at a time. They voted on the name, finishing options, everything. We created an entire line of sourced whiskey and they're part of every decision we make. They are seeing things that you'll only see doing it this way." They also educated the Tribe about the tradition of independent bottling. "We started saying, how about instead of sourcing and renaming? How about we independently bottle, so ya'll can get a single barrel from Balcones or a single barrel from Wyoming? They were the first to take a risk on us and we were just some yahoos that started a distillery."

Crowded Barrel is currently distilling a Half Irish Peated American Single Malt, all voted upon by the Tribe, which also voted to have Ty Phelps from Andalusia (see page 274) help them peat their own barley. "We're fully embedded in the whiskey community. It's incredibly open handed. I mean Ty helped us with this, Balcones helped us with all sorts of things, the Ironroot guys helped teach us how to blend. When we created the blend for the Texas Whiskey Festival, all three of them let us do it. They said, sure man, you can have my whiskey and blend it with god knows what," he said, laughing. The second batch of the Texas Whiskey Festival Alliance blend includes Ranger Creek, Lone Elm, and Treaty Oak.

Daniel told me that just for fun one day, they asked the Tribe to pick between different grains. When the voting was done, they took the percentage of the answers and made a twelve-grain mash bill to the exact specs of the poll question. "We named it The Amalgamation. We have two barrels of it right now and it is weird as fuck. And we told them that there's a very good chance this is going to taste like shit, because sometimes that happens when you make whiskey by committee. If it's terrible we're putting it in a bottle that we've already gotten label approval for that says 'Do Not Drink This Whiskey.'"

I love this story. I love the idea that there's a crowdsourced whiskey and that of all of the places this could have happened, it was here. Like I've said, Texas' biggest strength is the lack of tradition. Crowded Barrel is, without question, the most nontraditional distillery concept I've ever encountered. I can't wait to see the depths of their creativity as they continue to expand their Tribe.

I wanted to see what the members had to say and I think my favorite was Donald Chadeayne who said, "It's the community. It's their non-judgmental way of guiding newbies toward the almost unlimited number of great whiskeys out there. It's their support during trying times for their fellow Magnificent Bastard's. It's the fellowship."

Isn't that what we all look for in a community? A little bit of knowledge gained, trust garnered, and a hell of a lot of fun to be had? Jared Hempstedt, head distiller at Balcones, said, "They're such authentic, genuine human beings. They couldn't be more honest. They're excited, they love whiskey, and they love their community. I mean, they accidentally made it, like slipped on a banana peel and boom, community, but I honestly don't know anyone in this industry who is more passionate about whiskey."

CROWDED BARREL ALLIANCE SERIES—TEXAS WHISKEY FESTIVAL BLEND

Created by blending 29.4% Ironroot Bloody Butcher, 29.4%, Ironroot Special Purple Corn, 29.4% Balcones Mirador, and 11.8% Andalusia Stryker, aged 24 months; only 1,200 375ml bottles made.

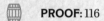 **PROOF:** 116

NOSE: The cigar you left on the patio because you just had to have pizza rolls and totally forgot you were halfway through a Cohiba, blackstrap molasses, sweet smells of a Starbucks lobby, a fresh cracked Dr. Pepper (not diet), and vanilla.

PALATE: Barrel spices, the part of the marshmallow that you've burnt to a crisp, old cowboy boots, French-pressed coffee, long lingering finish.

CROWDED BARREL

ALLIANCE SERIES

WHISKEY CO.

TEXAS WHISKEY FESTIVAL BLEND

BLENDED BOURBON WHISKEY

AGED 24 MOS.

BOTTLE NO.

DISTILLERS

IRONROOT REPUBLIC
BALCONES DISTILLING
ANDALUSIA WHISKEY CO

116 PROOF
375mL
58% ALC/VOL

A BLEND MADE UP OF 29.4% IRONROOT BLOODY BUTCHER
29.4% IRONROOT SPECIAL PURPLE, 29.4% BALCONES MIRADOR
AND 11.8% ANDALUSIA STRYKER

THIS IS TEXAS CRAFT.

WHAT IS THIS INDEPENDENT BOTTLING YOU SPEAK OF?

DANIEL WHITTINGTON

Whiskey drinkers don't need more sourced and rebranded whiskey with fake backstories and shady labeling practices. We don't need more retail house brands with vague origin stories and generic product descriptions. We need real distilleries making and sourcing and blending spirits they are proud of and acting with full transparency. And, frankly, we need more non-distillers featuring exclusive releases of well-known craft whiskeys. In short, America needs more independent bottlers. But what exactly is "independent bottling"?

Farmers and monasteries have distilled whisky in Scotland and Ireland since at least the 15th century, but commercial distilleries are almost as old. Whisky was localized until merchants like the Walkers, Dewars, and Buchanan began purchasing casks of whisky from distilleries and blending them to create specific flavor profiles. For convenience, we'll call them merchant blenders, although that is not an industry designation.

Eventually, to guarantee access, many of those blenders bought out the distilleries that produced the whisky they used in their blends. Even so, most of the retail product was a blend of multiple barrels from multiple distilleries. And those blends introduced the world to scotch whisky.

Eventually, after surviving two world wars, the Great Depression, and Prohibition in America, brands like Glenfiddich, Glenmorangie, and Macallan began to draw the world's attention to single malt whisky. (Reminder: single malt whisky is made from barley and distilled at one distillery.)

As the spotlight shifted from blends to single malt, a market opportunity emerged: hand-selected casks with limited releases from prized distilleries. We call the pioneers who took advantage of that opportunity independent bottlers. These companies purchased barrels from existing well-known distilleries and developed small-batch releases, often releasing a single barrel at a time.

It was a brilliant combination. If you knew and loved the distillery, you had the chance to try a rare release that was often very different from the standard core lines of your beloved bottlings. And if you fell in love with what was essentially a whisky curator, you could look at their other offerings and discover distilleries you may not have tried or even heard about.

Enter Gordon and MacPhail in the early 1800s: their success led to more independent releases. As the tradition grew, the next century brought us names that still stand today, like Cadenhead's, Berry Bros and Rudd, Adelphi, Signatory, Douglas Laing, Duncan Taylor, and many more.

But simply buying someone else's whiskey doesn't make you an independent bottler. There are a few key markers of independent bottlers in the UK that separate them from blenders, all of which involve transparency. First, the brand of the distillery and the bottler are both clearly announced on the bottle. For example, Signatory has its own branding, but they still display the origin distillery prominently on the front label. It's truly a cooperative effort. You will often find more detail, such as the bottle count and barrel aging details, and you're likely to experience cask strength whisky (or close to it) without filtering or coloring.

Independent bottlers are, truly, one of the best sources for unique releases from your favorite distillery. Unfortunately, the tradition didn't carry over to America. There is definitely a history of brands releasing whisky distilled by others, but it was never recognized in the same way as Gordon and MacPhail celebrated scotch. As far back as the late 1800s, Garvin Brown was purchasing whiskey from distillers, blending barrels together, and creating a brand that is still one of the strongest bourbon brands in the world, Old Forester.

The American approach is closer to Dewar's and Johnnie Walker, in that it's sourcing whiskey, and blending it for a specific flavor profile, and then releasing a stand-alone brand. In the UK they use names like blender or independent bottler, but in America it became referred to as "non-distiller producers" and it lacked the same cachet. It is, however, important to note that the lack of prestige in America is because of the loose connection with rectifiers and America's troubled history with them.

In the US, rectifiers took whiskey produced by distilleries and "rectified" it by changing it, adding flavoring, adding herbs, or even doctoring it into entirely different products. Sometimes the resulting product was good whiskey under another brand name, but, just as often, it was doctored to the point of being unrecognizable, or possibly even being dangerous to consume. Rectifiers were largely responsible for the backlash that prompted the Bottled-in-Bond act of 1897 and the Pure Food and Drug act of 1906.

In America, "sourcing" has become a dirty word in the world of whiskey and often results in a dubious response from whiskey aficionados. If you don't make it yourself, do you have any right to claim it as your own? Can you be proud of it? This affectation is particular to America, and the attitude is exacerbated by the fact that so many producers in recent years have outright lied or obfuscated the truth about their own whiskey. How many times have we seen brands talk about "the generations of family history" or "century-old family recipe" or something similar, only to find out they are buying whiskey from another distillery and bottling it as their own? Too many times.

However, as the world market of whiskey shrinks, more and more consumers are discovering independent bottlers from all over the world, including the US. They're garnering awards, introducing people to new distilleries, creating new products, and doing it all with honesty, integrity, and transparency. Frankly, it's about damn time.

In Texas, Crowded Barrel Whiskey was one of the first to produce an independent bottling under the umbrella of the Alliance Series. It's a true Signatory- or Cadenhead's-style release. We name the distillery, the aging, the distiller, and any details the distillery will let us share about the whiskey, and in doing so, we follow in the footsteps of so many others in the US that are brilliantly doing the same.

More of these companies are featuring American craft whiskey, including The Scotch Malt Whiskey Society, Single Cask Nation, and others. Most of these companies have their origins in bottling Scottish whiskey, but as the American craft and whiskey movement grows, they are expanding their offerings to include them. This development gives me hope for the future. It's a chance for you to explore curated whiskey through a brand with a similar love and palate as your own. Remember back when the only way to discover new music was through people like deejays and album reviewers? If you were like me, it didn't take long to find a person whose music preference so closely aligned with your own that you blindly trusted any recommendation they made.

That's what independent bottlers are for whiskey. They're whiskey curators. Start looking for them. Start tasting what they taste. Fall in love with their palates and choices. Discover the distilleries they feature. It's the golden age of whiskey drinking. Step up and grab a glass.

Daniel Whittington is one of the founders of Crowded Barrel Whiskey Company and one of the hosts of the Whiskey Tribe and the Whiskey Vault.

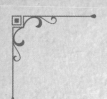

GARRISON BROTHERS DISTILLING

"I HAD A PARTNER EARLY ON and it was the "Garrison—[blank] Distillery. We had a divorce of sorts, basically I gave him a bunch of money to get the hell out of my life and it worked out for the better for both of us. But I had already ordered all these signs. I'd borrowed money from my mom, my dad, and brother to buy him out, so I was trying to save money and I had these signs, so I named it after my family. I was trying to be cheap," said Dan Garrison, owner and founder of Garrison Brothers Distilling.

Garrison Brothers is the original Texas bourbon, and was also the first whiskey maker in Texas. They should have been the first Texas whiskey released. "We were always going to make a straight bourbon. We were never going to release anything under two years old. But we broke that rule because this dude came along out of Waco, saying he was going to release the first whiskey. He aged his whiskey for about two weeks and then released it at a local liquor store. That really pissed me off. So we did a release of a one-year-old just to follow up because he beat us to market. He did. He didn't do it in a way that I thought was ethical, but he did. After that we made damn sure something like that would never happen again," recalled Garrison.

Garrison got his federal permit to distill alcohol and his state permit in 2007. "Back then, everything was done manually. You have to get two permits. The federal permit, and then you have to get a state permit to distill alcohol. The federal permit was a monster. Terrible pain in the ass to get through because there weren't even attorneys qualified to help because it had never been done before," he told me. "I submitted my paperwork to the Tax and Trade Bureau at least seventeen times. And every single time, they would send it back to me and say you missed a comma on page ten. You have to keep trying and hope that you're guessing correctly. Then comes phase two."

As Garrison put it, this is the part of the process that involves taking out ads in the local newspapers, talking to the county commissioners, talking to the local church leaders. You have to jump through a lot of different hoops to make sure they will approve your permit. "The only way you could have successfully filled out that application was to know the history of Prohibition in America. These documents were written in 1935. They haven't been updated, they haven't been modernized. Everything comes out of 1935 when the federal government gave up their jurisdiction over alcohol and pushed it to the states to figure it out on their own. As the states were wondering where to begin, some congressman who had previously worked on establishing Prohibition, wrote the rules, setting up the three-tier system."

During Prohibition, only pharmacies were permitted to sell alcohol. When you look at some of the bigger liquor stores across the nation, you'll see histories that include a conversion from drugstore to recreational drug store. "The industry here has only been around for fifteen, twenty years, so we don't have the influence that the wineries or breweries have. All our laws are backward. We're still living in these byzantine days of the 1930s. The laws were written to protect the retailers and the distributors, not the suppliers," explained Garrison.

Garrison went back and forth to Kentucky a dozen times over the first two years of his business. He was learning how stills were made, which ones made which spirit, how to operate a still, what's involved in the fermentation process, what grains ferment at different rates and temperatures, how to measure brix, how to measure the density of the spirit itself, and then he convinced his family to invest and convinced his mom to buy a plot of land out near Hye. "I bought it back about five years later," Garrison said with a laugh. "Those sixty-eight acres became Garrison Brothers Distillery, nestled in the heart of the Hill Country between Austin and Fredericksburg. At this point in time I had seven credit cards and $50,000 in debt, but thankfully I found some friends who were curious and helped invest a bit. Some of the funding for this came from a card game." By some, he means $1.9 million. "When I realized that the business would have to expand, after my wife and I had been funding and funding and funding it, I invited nine of my best friends to come out to the distillery to play cards and told them to bring their checkbooks. Next morning they left and they were investors in Garrison Brothers Distillery.

SOME SAY TEXANS
ARE A LITTLE TOO
PROUD OF THEIR STATE.

GARRISON
BROTHERS™
TEXAS STRAIGHT BOURBON WHISKEY

2019

BORN AND BRED IN HYE, TEXAS
47% ALC/VOL (94 PROOF)/750 ML

GARRISON
BROTHERS
Distillery

"God wanted me to make bourbon whiskey. I know this because one day I got a phone call and God was on the other end," Garrison said. "This wonderful woman who used to be the marketing director of Buffalo Trace called me and said 'I heard you were in Kentucky trying to learn whiskey.' And I said, 'Yes ma'am! I'm trying to learn how to make bourbon and Buffalo Trace has been great!' Two weeks later, I was on my way back up to Kentucky and I convinced her to meet me and she introduced me to some of the industry people she knew. I got to meet Max Shapira at Heaven Hill, I met Dave Pickerell and Bill Samuels at Maker's. She introduced me to Harlen Wheatley and Elmer T. Lee. It was incredible. All of these guys that I just looked up to as legends." Sure enough, two weeks later Dave Pickerell put in his notice at Maker's Mark. Garrison called him and said that while he didn't have much to offer, he'd pay for him to come down, offered up his RV for him to stay in, and promised he'd make him steaks and baked potatoes every night. "I just wanted him to tell me stories and show me how to operate this little still I had bought from Elmer T. Lee. And nobody knows more about distillation than Dave Pickerell. So, obviously, God wanted me to make bourbon whiskey. Dave was down for two weeks and it was the most magical two weeks of my life. I launched his consulting career. And I didn't pay him shit. But he didn't want that. That's what made him an amazing guy. He said, 'I'm just having a good time working with you, Dan.' It was an incredible couple of years with Dave as the angel on my shoulder, giving me advice on which direction to go with my company.

"I remember sitting with Dave Pickerell, and I had about four sheets of questions I wanted to ask him, and one of the questions was, 'What do you think the effect of year-round aging's going to be?' It hits 80 damn near twelve months a year and in the winter it's down into the 20s and sometimes lower. I said, 'How do you think that the aging environment is going to compare to what happens in Kentucky?' So Dave leans back in his chair, real slowly, and says, 'I can't wait to see it.' I kinda got the same thing with Elmer T. Lee when I asked him the same question. He goes, 'That could be very interesting.' And man, they knew, they knew that the honey barrels were in the hottest parts of the rickhouses."

When Garrison started, they had about forty different barrels, all with different mash bills, all with different char levels, all sorts of different cooperages, all aging to see which wound up ultimately being their product. Today, Small Batch is the same mash bill as the Single Barrel and the Cowboy and the Balmorhea. There are all sorts of experimental mash bills in the barns. Garrison calls Donnis

Todd, Garrison Brothers' head distiller, their de facto crazy man: "He's the mad scientist. There is a rye we'll be trying next year for the first time. Rye is typically a much more dense grain so it takes a longer time for the sweetness to come out of the grain and we knew it was going to take at least six years before we could release it. So I guess we'll see if there's any liquid left in the barrels. Donnis has them hidden, and he's going to bring them out when he thinks it's time to bring them out."

Garrison's old neighbor, Betsy, was the procurement director for Whole Foods Market. He always knew he wanted to be the first organic bourbon ever made. So he got Betsy to introduce him to Deaf Smith County Grain in Dalhart, Texas. "I literally loaded up my truck and drove up there, and asked the guy to throw in a couple of bags of their finest organic corn, yellow dent corn at the time. And they did, and it was converting about 18% of the sugar to alcohol during fermentation," said Dan. Then when he went back to buy more, he accidentally ended up with a truck load of white corn. "I wanted a yellow dent because that's what all the Kentucky growers had told me to use. I said, 'Can I return this stuff?' but I realized that the drive back to the Panhandle would cost more than actually just trying it. We tried it, and my first yield of my first batch yielded 22% sugar, and I liked the flavor of the white dog more with the yellow, so we switched to white corn." Needless to say, Garrison Brothers is wholly Texas grain to glass. He couldn't do it any other way. Originally, Garrison had 65 acres of organic soft red winter wheat planted on his land, but the challenges of being a farmer proved to be too much.

"We intend to stay small enough that we can taste each barrel to see what we like and what we don't," Garrison told me. "We taste every barrel at four years of age. And when we find a Cowboy barrel, it's going to be sweet, it's going to be crème de la crème of all the barrels that we're tasting that particular year. So we set those barrels aside. There's a secret location, called the honey spot, for those barrels and nobody gets to know about it except for Donnis. I don't even know where these barrels are hidden. That Cowboy Bourbon is uncut, it's unfiltered, and it's right out of the barrel."

When you step onto the grounds of Garrison Brothers, you know it's special. Polarizing whiskey be damned, the ranch is the stuff legends are made of. It's pristine, it's masculine, but soft enough to be approachable and you can feel a certain calm that is singular to that place. This is the original Texas whiskey, and we could not be luckier to have them on our Mount Rushmore. Dan Garrison is one of the reasons that Texas whiskey is where it is today thanks to his brash, unapologetic commitment to his product and making it exactly the way he sees fit. "I think Texas is the next great whiskey state. I think that the products coming out of Texas currently are far superior to anything being produced in Kentucky today. And I'm saying this publicly, fully expecting the wrath of Khan from Kentucky, but I mean it. This is the next haven for bourbon whiskey, the great state of Texas." Yee haw, y'all.

SMALL BATCH TEXAS STRAIGHT BOURBON

This is the one you'll see all over, the flagship, the torch bearer, the first Texas bourbon, made of 74% Texas white corn, 15% wheat, and 11% barley.

PROOF: 94

NOSE: Rotisserie chicken, buckwheat honey, honeysuckle, newly mowed backyard, Orange Julius.

PALATE: Buttered pound cake, old-fashioned orange slice candy, Christmas spices, the Texas State Fair midway, sugar cookies, very long finish of chocolate-covered espresso beans and toasted oak.

TEXAS STRAIGHT BOURBON SINGLE BARREL

Single barrel version of the Small Batch; from their website: "Visitors can buy a bottle of the Single Barrel that they bottle themselves at the distillery. They can also select their own barrel, bottle the barrel with friends and family, and purchase the bottles and empty barrel at their liquor store of choice."

PROOF: 94

NOSE: Almond toffee, chopped vanilla bean, grass, roasted pork butt, spent fireworks.

PALATE: Sweet oak, nutmeg and cinnamon, unsweetened cocoa powder, hot apple cider, burnt sugar, hazelnut, hint of arroz con leche.

BALMORHEA

A straight bourbon aged 4 years in new American white oak barrels and then transferred to a second new American white oak barrel and aged an additional year.

PROOF: 114

NOSE: Amaretto Disaronno, Nutella, caffe mocha, crushed red pepper.

PALATE: Old Port (like from before 1970), triple-chocolate caramel-fudge brownies, Knack (Swedish Christmas butterscotch), hot chili oil, cigar box.

HONEYDEW

Garrison Small Batch, infused with Burleson's Texas Wildflower Honey; head distiller Donnis Todd transformed used bourbon barrels into small wooden cubes that were immersed in honey and those were used to infuse the bourbon for 7 months.

PROOF: 80

NOSE: Soaked honeycomb, Fredericksburg peaches off the vine, toasted almond, cream soda.

PALATE: Coffee ice cream, tobacco leaf, Applewood-smoked chipotle chilis, grilled peaches, white chocolate-covered espresso beans, lingering bright finish with umistakable taste of honey.

COWBOY BOURBON

This was Jim Murrary's American Whiskey of the Year in 2014 and 2017; this is essentially a hand-selected barrel blend set aside from honey barrels for another couple of years of maturation that is kept at cask strength.

PROOF: 133.9

NOSE: Extinguished campfire, cedar sap, burnt dulce de leche, sugar beet molasses.

PALATE: Incredibly oily, burned molasses, homemade apple crumb with caramel on top, smoked fig, Caffe del Fuego, roasted walnut, suede leather, buckwheat honey.

HYE RYE

The color is deep amber and almost like eucalyptus honey in Garrison's first exploration of high-rye bourbon, which has been aged 5 years; the mash bill is 52% corn, 37% rye, and 11% barley. This is a very limited release only available from the distillery.

 PROOF: 98

 NOSE: Spiced cherries, raisins, leather, orange blossoms.

 PALATE: Waves of baking spices with sweet hints of molasses, caramel, and vanilla, with a buttery finish of clove, cinnamon, ginger, and warm sorghum.

DAN GARRISON: IN HIS OWN WORDS

Garrison Brothers Distillery began as an entrepreneurial fantasy in 2001. The software company I helped build collapsed as a casualty of the Enron scandal. I believe 12,000 Texans lost their jobs and their life savings in 2001. At forty years of age, I was one of them.

Looking at the newspaper one night in bed next to my wife Nancy, I read her a story about yet another Texas distillery planning to make vodka. Since she was a vodka drinker, and I think I'm funny, I asked, "Why would anyone want to make vodka? It has no flavor and no taste. Why doesn't someone make something that actually tastes good, like bourbon?" She replied, "As much of that stuff as you drink, maybe you should. We'd probably save money." That hit home. Hard.

Two weeks later, I was visiting the Kentucky Bourbon Trail with notebook in hand. At the time, there were only nine companies making all thirty-five of the bourbon brands on liquor store shelves. The reality was that bourbon had become unpopular; it was grandaddy's drink. And of the thirty-five brands being made about two-thirds of them were variations on the real deal. There was Wild Turkey 80 proof and Wild Turkey 101 proof. Jim Beam, Knob Creek, Basil Hayden's, and Bookers are all just older or stronger versions of Jim Beam. Jack Black and Jack Daniels Green Label were the exact same juice, just in different colored bottles. Other than the bottle shape, is Old Forester truly different from Woodford Reserve?

In seeing through these thinly-veiled marketing efforts I recognized an opportunity to create something truly new, unique, and authentic. Thus began my journey down bourbon road. But I did not walk it alone. Dave Pickerell, the Master Distiller at Maker's Mark for fifteen years walked alongside me. Elmer T. Lee, before he passed, gave me nuggets for my recipe and cook procedures. Craig Beam walked me through the Louisville-based Old Forester plant. Chris Morris showed me how Woodford Reserve came to be at the Labrot and Graham Distillery in Versailles, Kentucky. These men became mentors and friends who I still admire today.

In 2003, I convinced my mother-in-law to acquire a majestic 68-acre parcel of Texas Hill Country. I moved in and brought my copper still along with me. In 2006, I convinced Mike and Rob Sherman at Vendome Brass and Copper Works to sell me Elmer T. Lee's 100-gallon experimental still, which Harlen Wheatley had replaced with a more modern version. She (the Copper Cowgirl) and I spent many nights drinking together as she made more bourbon for us to enjoy. In 2007, I applied for a federal permit to distill alcohol. After numerous submissions, the Tax and Trade Bureau granted me a distiller's permit. A month later the state of Texas did as well. Suddenly, I owned and operated the first legal whiskey distillery in Texas history, and the first 100% pure bourbon distillery outside of Kentucky.

Straight bourbon whiskey matters. Good bourbon helps celebrate important milestones in one's life. Good bourbon creates lasting friendships. Good bourbon fuels legendary stories like my own. Good bourbon can change the world. I am witness to it every day.

Today, I have the greatest job on earth. After almost twenty years, my business now offers roughly seven straight bourbon whiskey brands. Each is unique and can stand up on its own. We cannot even fulfill the orders we receive from distributors and retailers and we decline most inquiries. Our bourbons are regarded as the best in the world. I get to drink good bourbon with new friends every night all over the world.

Some day soon we are going to turn a profit and show those sons of bitches who said it can't be done.

MAVERICK WHISKEY

KEN MAVERICK HAS LONG BEEN INTERESTED in his family history. When your great-great-great grandfather was one of the original signers of the Texas Declaration of Independence, how could you not be? As the story goes, Samuel Maverick was at The Alamo but rode out on a mission to Washington-on-the-Brazos to round up help a couple of days before the slaughter. He left the fellas a jug of whiskey, however. We do know for certain that Samuel Maverick was one of the most crucial figures in the history of San Antonio and that he and his family owned tens of thousands of acres of land, including the eventual site of Lockwood National Bank. Fun fact: Lockwood was the first bank in Texas to allow women to deposit money, which was vital in a town with a thriving red-light district.

After a small incident in his basement while home distilling, which caused the entire house to reek, Amy, Maverick's wife and distillery co-owner, told her husband to find a new place to distill. In 2017, they bought the building on the corner of their family's old homestead and founded Maverick Whiskey. After two years of renovations, Maverick Whiskey is now establishing their own history as a key piece of a revitalized downtown San Antonio. "We wanted to create a unique experience for San Antonians and those who come to visit our city," Amy told me. "We also want to leave this for our children and keep it in the family for generations to come so that it's down here telling this story even when we are long gone from San Antonio."

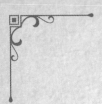
Everything coming out of Maverick Whiskey is completely Texas grain to glass. I can also safely say that they are the only distillery in Texas that is aging their whiskey in a bank fault. Head distiller Rikk Munroe told me, "The city made us ventilate it, for good reason. It's actually a few degrees within ambient temperature outside, which is great because you're getting that temperature fluctuation both daily and seasonally. Our rickhouse just happens to be a concrete bunker." They also use 30-gallon barrels because the city of San Antonio wouldn't allow them to have anything larger in the vault.

Munroe told me a funny story about how he walked into the distillery one day and one of his assistants was just about finished pouring the grain into the mash tun and he said "Wait, that's not wheat." As it turns out, it was triticale, but since it was already in there, they went ahead and distilled it. They're keeping an eye on this accident and hopefully it turns into a happy one.

Maverick's Alamo Whiskey is a grain-forward whiskey distilled from a Maverick family mash bill, aged for one day. They also have a one-year Light Whiskey and their current Straight Bourbon is a sourced Texas whiskey while they age their own distillate so they can release their bank-vault aged bourbon and rye whiskey. And you can take that to the bank! (I'm sorry...)

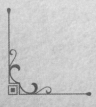

TEXAS STRAIGHT BOURBON WHISKEY

This namesake whiskey is a high-rye bourbon that is non-chill filtered and aged a minimum of 2 years.

PROOF: 88

NOSE: Sweet black tea, soda fountain cola, buttermilk caramel cake.

PALATE: Crème brûlée, stone fruit, Coquito, peppery cinnamon with a touch of menthol.

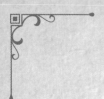
MILAM & GREENE WHISKEY

IF YOU'RE NOT FAMILIAR WITH THE BOOK *Whiskey Distilled* by Heather Greene, and you find yourself enjoying this tale of Texas whiskey, *Whiskey Distilled* is one of my favorite introductions to this subject. Greene has an amazing ability to convey the technical aspects of whiskey, inundating you with facts, but also makes everything digestible in a very candid manner. Her voice is approachable and informative. She has a certain ease in the way she teaches her readers the different ways to approach whiskey.

Greene was the first woman to serve on the Scotch Malt Whisky Society tasting panel, and is currently on additional tasting panels, and was recently inducted into the inaugural class of the Order of the Writ. But for our purposes, the most important fun fact about her is that she, finally, has her own distillery. Greene left the friendly confines of New York City and moved to Texas in 2019 to serve as the CEO of Ben Milam Whiskey in Blanco. The company is now Milam & Greene Whiskey, with Greene joining serial entrepreneur Marsha Milam (who originally named the company after Ben Milam, a Texas revolutionary and distant relative) and head distiller Marlene Holmes, who spent twenty-seven years distilling in various capacities at Jim Beam.

I feel like this is the part of the book where I should talk about the importance of women in the distilling industry, and I feel like I should make note that this is the only distillery in the state owned only by women. Needless to say, Greene, Milam, and Holmes are changing the face of Texas whiskey and it was such a joy to spend an afternoon in a place with both incredible whiskey and a lack of machismo. Instead of asking the predictable question "How is it being a woman in this industry?" I asked Holmes what it was like to join a company with all female decision makers. She replied, "It was one of the reasons that brought me here. I wanted an opportunity to have a seat at the table. It's been incredible."

They were recently honored at the San Francisco World Spirits Competition with Double Gold medals for their Straight Rye Whiskey Finished in Port Wine Casks and their Barrel Proof Straight Bourbon. "I first came down as a consultant and just thought there was something here. I just loved this team and I loved the inventory of the whiskey they were aging and the flavor already coming off the still. Something felt right about it," Greene told me. "There was this Texas aspect to it. Texas has a renegade spirit about it that lends itself to experimentation. There's a 'I'm gonna do what I want' attitude and as a whiskey maker, that's exciting. The other thing is that, frankly, we don't even know what these possibilities are. We know Kentucky and Tennessee, for example, make phenomenal whiskies, 53-gallon barrels, four years, and we know what to expect, but here we get to find out. I love the mystery of it. There are a lot of people who say Texas whiskey is this, this, and this. I'm not willing to say that. I don't think we know what it is yet. I think it's going to take some time. Ten years, in the history of whiskey, is nothing. This is a giant state. We should really be thinking more about this in less of a macro way. The physicality of geography does not know arbitrary governmental boundaries."

This, my friends, is a damn fine point. I've seen this visceral reaction to Texas whiskey by bourbon heads who won't even try it because they think it will suck because it isn't aged for at least four years. Why four years? Because everyone who was making whiskey at the time in the similar climates of Kentucky and Tennessee were all coming to the conclusion that four years was about right? Because they were first and because they helped make bourbon a legally American spirit, but they only had their own processes to quantify? Because eighteen-month-old Kentucky whiskey is terrible, so it must be that way everywhere else? There are more arbitrary regulations and categorizations in whiskey than you can shake a stick at.

"I've never seen whiskey as just the raw ingredients and the process," Greene told me. "Whiskey is made by people and it drives me nuts when you define whiskey purely by grains, or just how you distill it, or just how you age it. Whiskey to me is a lens of something much bigger."

What differentiates Greene's specific approach from the majority of other whiskey makers in Texas is her focus on variety. Milam & Greene has focused on both transparently batching and blending sourced products and creating grain-to-glass Certified Texas Whiskey products.

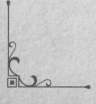

"I think it's okay to source, but I think you have to say you're sourcing it and be very clear about what you're doing to define yourself as a whiskey from your state. I disagree with a lot of people here. 'What makes a whiskey from that place?' is the big question, and it's yet to be truly answered. To me, transparency is a strength. If you have the ability to get a hold of amazing whiskey and blend it into something unique, that's absolutely something that you should talk about. That's a good thing right?" Greene said with a laugh. "Why wouldn't I use everything I can to create something beautiful?"

Greene told me that she still wants Holmes to distill in Kentucky on the massive stills that she has gotten to know the past three decades. Because of her friends there, Holmes was able to take the Milam & Greene mash bill she helped create to Kentucky to do some runs. Afterward, Greene said, "They brought them back in totes, which means it's whiskey, but not bourbon. Bourbon doesn't exist until you put white whiskey into new charred American oak, as you know. So this didn't become bourbon until it was in Texas. And then it's going to age here for four years. So, what is that? Is that a Kentucky whiskey? Is that a Texas bourbon?

"One of the things that I think is incredibly important is not to ask 'Did you?' but to ask 'How did you?' How did you harness the Texas terroir into your whiskey? Not did you distill or did you not because, for instance, the answer to that with our triple cask is yes. We distilled and we didn't distill. When you get deeper into questions about provenance or terroir and what it is to be a whiskey and if you're only looking at it through the tiny lens of distillation, you forget all of the things that happen before and after that point in the process. I just think it's more complicated than that."

So when you have a Texas mash bill, distilled in Kentucky by a now Texas distiller, immediately brought back to Texas without becoming bourbon until it comes to Texas, and then it sits in Hill Country to age for four years, some say this is absolutely not Texas whiskey. Heather Greene says how in the world could it be anything else?

GRAIN TO GLASS, 1ˢᵀ EDITION

This first grain-to-glass bourbon from Milam & Greene is 70% corn, 22% malted rye, 8% malted barley, and 100% Texas; only 7 barrels of this were made and it's only available at the distillery.

PROOF: 121.9

NOSE: Honey cake, iced gingerbread cookie, roasted walnuts, lemon ricotta, nutmeg, light esters.

PALATE: Roasted poblano pepper, smoked pecans, figs in a balsamic reduction, super short on the front of your palate, lingers in the back of your throat.

STRAIGHT BOURBON

This is Tennessee-sourced and has no age statement, but it's 4 to 5 years old; it took home a Double Gold at the San Francisco Spirits Competition.

PROOF: 86

NOSE: Brown sugar, caramel apple, roasted peanuts, English toffee.

PALATE: Atomic Fireball up front, pumpkin spice, touch of sawdust, turbinado sugar, crisp and clean, buttery-smooth finish.

RYE WHISKEY

A delightful blend of 3-, 4-, and 6-year-old casks from MGP that is aged additionally in the volatile Hill Country climate; there is also a port barrel-finished version that's badass.

PROOF: 90.4

NOSE: Crème brûlée, Cinnamon Imperials candy, toasted oak, baker's chocolate, blackberry jam.

PALATE: Mulled apples with nutmeg, cracked black pepper, allspice, velvety on the tongue, vanilla bean.

TRIPLE CASK
BLENDED BOURBON

This is a blend of straight bourbon whiskies—2-year-old Texas bourbon, a 3- to 4-year-old Tennessee whiskey, and 10- to 11-year-old Tennessee whiskey—made with 70% Texas corn, 22% Pacific Northwest malted rye, 8% Wyoming barley, and their proprietary yeast recipe from Kentucky and Texas.

PROOF: 94

NOSE: White grapes, red bell pepper, ambrosia salad, newly mowed grass on the first day of baseball season.

PALATE: Cinnamon rock candy, paprika, dried tobacco leaf, vanilla custard, mincemeat pie.

The Five Star is the brainchild of Justin Lavenue, co-owner of the celebrated cocktail bar The Roosevelt Room, and its neighboring bar and event space, The Eleanor, located in downtown Austin.

1¼ oz. Milam & Greene Port Cask Finished Rye Whiskey

¾ oz. reposado tequila (preferably El Tesoro or Siembra Azul)

¼ oz. cinnamon syrup

2 dashes Peychaud's Bitters

2 dashes mole bitters

1. Combine all of the ingredients, except the lemon peel, in an Old Fashioned glass, place one large ice cube in the glass, and then stir slowly, being careful not to get the top of the ice cube wet.

2. Garnish with a lemon peel.

RANGER CREEK BREWING & DISTILLING

I'VE SPENT MY ENTIRE LIFE AS AN ENTREPRENEUR. Some projects have been successful, some have been terrible, terrible ideas, but all of them have been... a massive amount of work. I've always liked the idea that entrepreneurs are all, in their own way, change agents. The road to entrepreneurship is chock-full of roadblocks and dead-ends. It's rewarding, but it also requires relentless focus.

The entrepreneurial spirit in Texas whiskey is one of the industry's hallmarks. Like I've said, Texas doesn't have a storied history of whiskey makers. Those who have dared to venture out into this chaos have all come from different paths, and while they all have led to whiskey, they sure as hell weren't planning on that direction. When you have yet to write history, there are very few who want to join you as you attempt to do so. Ranger Creek Brewing & Distilling is indisputably rooted in entrepreneurship.

The idea for Ranger Creek was born when three home brewers, and future business partners, TJ Miller, Dennis Rylander, and Mark McDavid decided that San Antonio needed a brewery and a distillery. Ranger Creek started in 2010 as the first production brewery in San Antonio of the modern era and one of the first three Texas whiskey distilleries. "We entered our beer in a competition in Houston and won a couple of gold medals and around the same time the three of us went to tour Kentucky and we kept asking ourselves why no one was doing this in Texas. At this time there was no proof that we could even make whiskey in Texas," said Rylander. "In 2009, we raised enough to order our equipment and all of a sudden we were in business. It was really overnight that we went from having a hobby to having a company. It was exhilarating and terrifying all at the same time."

"The biggest difference between us and other breweries that add on distilling capabilities is that we aren't set up to do single malts, we're set up to do bourbon," said Miller. "We distill on the grain every time." There are a million difficulties when you're dealing directly with the grain and it makes all of the sense in the world to not want to tackle it when you have an option to not. From the beginning, Ranger Creek was going to do their best to create the highest quality product with a focus on specificity. While they may have followed successful breweries turned distilleries like Dogfish Head or Rogue, they wanted to make bourbon from the jump.

In the opinion of Ranger Creek, the barrel is the most important element to making whiskey. "The barrel is where the magic is," Rylander said. When they began their journey, they started with five different cooperages, five different sizes, and five different char levels. They wanted to be able to explore the impact of the Texas environment as thoroughly as possible. In 2015, Ranger Creek's .36 Single Barrel won Best of Show in the American Craft Spirits Association competition, an award that Balcones won the year before.

One of my favorite things about Ranger Creek is their whiskey club. It's a replica of wine clubs you may have seen out there, but it's shockingly innovative in the whiskey world. "There are some laws on the books in Texas that don't allow for distilleries to ship direct to the consumer, but we started the club with the hope that would change one day," said Rylander. So as of now, you have to come by the distillery to pick up the whiskey allocated to the club members, which is fine. Texans are always down for a road trip. Club members have first access to limited-release whiskeys and there are special bottlings that are only available to members.

With their use of 375 ml bottles, the whiskey club has always served as a source of creativity. They're able to experiment with different finishing casks, with different grains, hell with different types of spirits on occasion. I asked Rylander which of the experiments was the most out there and he said without a doubt it was their brisket whiskey: "We partnered with a local restaurant and we did a whiskey infusion with the brisket. It was quite involved, and incredible in different ways. It literally tasted like a liquid brisket, which is good and bad. It tasted great, but it was also like drinking a brisket, which, for me, wasn't something I was wanting to do. Thankfully, we found out that putting it in a Bloody Mary was the best combination ever. We got a lot of press and everyone seemed to love it. It was just about as extreme as you can go with a whiskey, in my opinion."

Ranger Creek has always been one of the loudest voices in the fight for transparency. They caused a huge stink in the world of Texas whiskey in late 2014 when they posted a blog about Makers vs. Fakers when it came to those operating grain to glass in Texas and those simply sourcing but using words to make you believe the product was made entirely in Texas. If you'd like to read the blog in its entirety, feel free to buy my other book, *Texas Cocktails*. See? Told ya I'm an entrepreneur. #HustleHard.

.36 CASK STRENGTH

The flagship version of their flagship bourbon, this grain to glass Texas bourbon is aged in 5- to 10-gallon barrels; ages and proofs vary, but the one I sampled was aged for 2 years and 2 months.

PROOF: 121.6

NOSE: Vanilla and maple syrup with newly toasted oak, sweet corn muffin.

PALATE: Strong caramel, newly cut 2X4, cinnamon, warm and spicy on the short finish.

RANGER CREEK

.36
CASK
STRENGTH

TEXAS STRAIGHT
BOURBON WHISKEY

LIMITED EDITION

Bottle # : 1002   Alc/Vol: 63.6 Proof.

Aged under the Texas sun for: 2yrs 3 mo

RIMFIRE

The mash bill used is actually Ranger Creek's Mesquite Smoked Porter beer, sans the hops, which is made from 5 different barley varietals; a true American single malt, aged in ex-Ranger Creek bourbon barrels lightly smoked with Texas mesquite. Grain to glass and a member of their "Small Caliber" series, which comes in 375 ml bottles; my sample bottle was aged 23 months in super barrels.

PROOF: 86

NOSE: Tropical notes including mango and banana, hint of charred cedar plank (like those fancy bros do at cocktail bars).

PALATE: Slightly smokey, dried apricot, peach cobbler, malt comes through with a chocolatey finish.

300 SMOKED SINGLE MALT

Created to honor the 300th Anniversary of San Antonio, this single malt whiskey was smoked with beechwood and aged in Freetail's La Muerta barrels, which is a stout brewed each year for Día de los Muertos.

PROOF: 86

NOSE: Newly lit campfire, peach cobbler, Basque Burnt Cheesecake, grilled mango.

PALATE: Smoke, a little thin, chocolate-covered malted milk balls, honey, chocolate wafers, dates, warm and slightly smokey, root beer on the finish.

.44 RYE

100% rye whiskey aged in used Ranger Creek bourbon barrels; one of the best rye whiskeys in Texas, available in 375 ml bottles with varying age statements. My sample bottle was aged in small barrels for 23 months.

 PROOF: 94

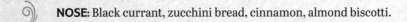 **NOSE:** Black currant, zucchini bread, cinnamon, almond biscotti.

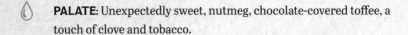 **PALATE:** Unexpectedly sweet, nutmeg, chocolate-covered toffee, a touch of clove and tobacco.

TEXAS RYE–TEJAS EDITION

The first Tejas Edition collaboration between the Texas Whiskey Festival and a single Texas distiller, it's a 2 ½-year-old rye, finished in an Austin Eastciders barrel; only 258 bottles were produced and are only available at the distillery.

PROOF: 94

NOSE: Crisp fresh apple and touches of honey, light and airy.

PALATE: Floral, musty wood, stewed cinnamon apple compote, if you squint there's a hint of mint.

.36 PORT CASK FINISH

A distillery-only release available to members of the Texas Whiskey Club, finished in white port barrels, unlike most of the port barrel finished you'll find; another member of the "Small Caliber" series.

PROOF: 94

NOSE: Oak spice, hints of plum, roasted black grapes on toasted baguette.

PALATE: Dutch dark chocolate, candied cherries, blackberry syrup, spiced hot fruit bake.

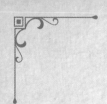

REAL SPIRITS

REAL ALE HAS BEEN MAKING UNFILTERED, unpasteurized beer in Hill Country since the 1990s. They're one of the original craft breweries in Texas and started in the basement of an antique store in Blanco. After over twenty years, Brad Farbstein, owner of Real Ale, started dabbling with distillation and in 2017 Real Spirits was launched. Nowadays Davin Topel, formerly of High West Distillery, heads up the production and operations.

All Real Spirits start with Real Ale beer. Currently, Topel is using a combination of Real Ale's Belgian-style Tripel and Real Heavy Scotch Ale to make their Signature and Single Barrel whiskeys, both of which are fully Texas grain to glass. The brewers make these beers in exactly the same manner as usual, but abstain from adding hops. "I was very fortunate working with a distiller who was a brewer before he was a distiller and understood what yeast does to different beer styles with regard to flavor. Yeast is incredibly important to us. We don't distill bad beer just because it's bad beer." Not surprisingly, the process is cyclical, as Real Ale uses these barrels to age beers.

Real Spirits uses a good old-fashioned Texas rickhouse, multiple shipping containers firmly planted behind the brewery. Topel says he's seeing about the same amount of aging in two years in the Hill Country as you would find in about four years in a place like Kentucky. The variance in temperature and the dramatic swings are what make aging whiskey in the Hill Country so unique.

While not whiskey, if you find yourself at Real Spirits, you need (yes, need) to check out their Totem. Topel loves mezcal, so he adopted the distillation style of *pechuga* to create this entirely unique spirit. For those unfamiliar, pechuga is sort of a gin made out of agave. You take a spirit and add botanicals that are indigenous to your area and put them in the still while taking a large protein (typically rooster or turkey) and suspending it over the still, where the vapors cook the meat and the drippings drop into the distillate. Topel used Fredricksburg peaches, Blanco lavender, berries, and bottlebrush leaves sourced from Real Ale's property to go along with a hog that was hunted and harvested from the Lockhart area. Vegans, steer clear.

SINGLE MALT DOUBLE BARREL

This second release of Double Barrel Whiskey starts as a mash of Real Ale's Real Heavy Scotch Ale and relies on a complex malt bill including caramalt, chocolate malt, and peated malt; twice distilled and aged in new charred white oak barrels for seventeen months, then transferred into a port barrel from Grape Creek Vineyards for 4 months.

PROOF: 92

NOSE: Baking spices, cinnamon, maple syrup, oatmeal cookies.

PALATE: Sweet dried fruit, chocolate macaroon, a touch of sawdust, and hint of smoke and leather.

RYE GRAIN STRAIGHT MALT WHISKEY

With a mash bill of 85% malted barley and 15% malted rye, there's a spicy and bold complexity that complements the sweet toasted cereal vibe of the barley in this very cool and unique whiskey.

PROOF: 100

NOSE: Maple, toasted oak, Tajín-covered dry mangos.

PALATE: Sweet caramel, toasted cereal grains, malted milk balls, Spanish hot chocolate and churros.

TEXAS HILL COUNTRY WHISKEY

Made from a combination of Real Ale's Devil's Backbone, their Belgian-style Tripel, and their Heavy Scotch Ale (exclusive of any hops), this single malt is twice-pot distilled and aged for nearly 2 years in charred new American oak barrels. Damn near chuggable.

PROOF: 90

NOSE: Banana pudding, vanilla buttercream frosting, *capirotada*.

PALATE: Fresh pipe tobacco, baking spices, light oak, baked apple, buttery, slight vanilla note.

FROM BEER TO WHISKEY

DAVIN TOPEL

As most already know, the mash is the starting point for all whiskey. Whiskey is defined as "a spirit distilled from grain," and, as all beer is made up predominantly of barley, all whiskey starts as a beer. Now, it's not traditional drinking beer for multiple reasons, most notably because a distiller's beer is un-hopped. While hops create some beautifully complex flavors in beer, they do not translate the same through a still. Another difference, at least in the US, is that most distiller's beer has not gone through the lautering process, which is straining out the grain matter before heading into fermentation. The final difference is that distiller's beer is most commonly inoculated with a distiller's yeast. This is a specific species of yeast (*Saccharomyces cerevisiae*) that has a particularly strong ability to metabolize sugar and produce alcohol as a by-product. Distiller's yeast also has a major impact on the flavor of your final spirit. Depending on what kind of whiskey you are making, the distiller's beer can contribute from 20% to 50% of the final flavor profile.

While the fermented wash that goes into a still is only technically a beer; it's not the sort of thing you'd find at a store or want to pull from a tap. However, a number of distillers in recent years have realized that a fine whiskey can get a head start when it's made from a fine beer. Some have even formed partnerships with craft breweries to source the liquid they will eventually distill. At Real Spirits, we started with an in-house advantage. With twemty-five years of experience producing award-winning beers, in a variety of styles, several of those beers perfectly lend themselves to crafting flavorful whiskeys.

Some of the benefits working with a brewery are that the yeast and grain handling are taken care of, but the most important is having brewers on your team with a wealth of knowledge on how to create well-balanced and flavorful beers. This translates extremely well into our whiskey.

At Real Ale, naturally, we focus a lot of our attention on yeast. We are very particular with the different yeasts we use to achieve several different flavor profiles and we have a full staff of talented chemists that make sure our yeast is healthy and happy. These chemists have created several sensory programs that help us identify desirable flavor profiles as well as helping to pinpoint "off flavors" that can be produced between the brewing and fermenting process.

An example of utilizing a brewer's yeast, as opposed to a distiller's yeast, for flavor, would be the mash we make from our Belgium Trippel, Devil's Backbone. The beer is made from 100% two-row malted barley and fermented with a Belgium yeast strain that produces flavors of banana and clove and these same esters produce a unique quality in the whiskey.

Another benefit to working at a brewery is having the means to lauter off the grain material before fermentation, which is common in scotch whisky production, but unusual in American distilling. By taking out all the extra grain matter, you are able to extract some unnecessary tannins that are caused by the boiling process in the still. It's similar to steeping tea in hot water for too long – you end up with a bitter, astringent cup.

Our distiller's beer boils for four to six hours and if there are still husks, some of those tannins would normally come through, but with our lautering process, this is no longer a factor. We end up with a much softer whiskey going into the barrel. You will, of course, pick up some natural tannins from the barrel, but this is desirable for body and structure and ends up yielding an extremely smooth whiskey.

To me, it's only natural for a brewery to start distilling. Much like the vineyards and wine producers in France distilling brandy, it is a logical progression. If you are crafting a great product, why not make another that is altogether new and appealing? If you are a brewery, all you need is a still and someone with a good palate to run it.

Davin Topel is the head distiller at Real Spirits and works in concert with Real Ale to create their line of whiskeys made from various expressions of their beers.

TREATY
OAK
DISTILLING

GHOST HILL

118

9/22/19

#1737

TREATY OAK

I CAN'T REMEMBER WHAT TOOK ME THERE, but I absolutely remember visiting the first version of Treaty Oak, back in 2006, in an industrial area of Austin. Daniel Barnes, founder and CEO of Treaty Oak, opened the fourth distillery operating in Texas. He'll tell you himself that they managed to only catch on fire twice, which isn't bad, considering the homemade pot-style still was an open-fire turkey fryer. While always intending to move into whiskey, Barnes somehow managed to distill the first gin and the first rum in Texas

Now, Treaty Oak sits on a 28-acre ranch outside of Dripping Springs that not only holds their operations but also has an open-air cocktail bar, a cocktail lab (including a RotoVap, condenser, and centrifuge) and an awesome restaurant called Alice's, which is named after Barnes's mom. Treaty Oak is one of the two original companies to stake their claim on Fitzhugh Road, which is now so inundated with craft beverage makers, justifying the town's nickname of "Drinking Springs."

One of my favorite stories about Treaty Oak is the story of their Red Handed Whiskey. In an effort to be transparent, this whiskey is named to make sure that the consumer knows that Treaty Oak has been "caught red handed" stealing someone else's whiskey. This is a sourced 2-year-old Straight Kentucky Bourbon Whiskey from Heaven Hill. Their other sourced product is their Schenley Reserve Rye, which is a 10-year sourced rye from the Schenley Distillery in Canada, which no longer exists (so buy all you can if it's your jam).

Treaty Oak is a true Texas grain-to-glass distillery. In fact, the grain portion of their operation is just about as local you can get. They sold a portion of the distillery property to James Brown, who owns Barton Springs Mill, where Treaty Oak buys their milled grain. Part of the sale was focused around Barton Springs Mill building out a new malting floor, so all of the malted barley Treaty Oak uses can be milled 100 yards from the distillery. Brown was actually crucial to introducing Treaty Oak to farmers who would be able to help achieve their goals of working with 100% Texas grown grains. Treaty Oak has always been community focused and now their focus on sustainability is a new extension of those ideals. Enter, Jamie Biel, Director of Science and Sustainability.

"Sustainability is a common thread through everything we do," Biel told me. "We have somewhere around forty employees nationwide. Sustainability is about being able to keep eyes on every single piece of the supply chain. It's about being able to keep true to our ethos of giving back, not just to the employees but the community. It means specifically helping those in the community who have been marginalized. And with COVID-19, we needed to find ways to help those who had been furloughed and make sure they were still being taken care of. Sustainability is much more than just environmental stewardship. There's a huge component that is about social and emotional wellness."

Since Biel has come on, there have been massive changes in the standard operating procedures in the supply chain of Treaty Oak. With sustainability being the primary focus. She spoke with the farmers who grow their grain, talking about water input and output on site, trying to close as many loops as possible, trying to meld their systems with the other systems that they were using, even if it wasn't their execution. "Any sustainability initiative that you want to put into place will have a financial impact that will prove to be cash positive within X number of years. Sustainability is fiscally responsible in the long run. I had to learn how to speak the language of business and present the reason to work toward sustainability from a business perspective. The next step was to start to implement some of the more feasible projects. My absolute favorite was the garden," said Biel.

Barnes wanted Alice's to use as much on-site produce as possible. Biel was charged with designing and physically building a 5000-square-foot organic garden. After initially learning to make the best use of the well water the property has on site, Biel designed and built out a rainwater collection system. What they have now is a beautiful, seasonally-focused garden that is one of the highlights of any visit to the ranch.

"Being sustainable is not easy. It sounds cute but it's difficult. It's expensive. It's the right way to do it, but it's going to be harder. The challenge in our industry, and everywhere else, is to change our perspective about business and put longevity over profit while also realizing that profit is ultimately tied to sustaining your company. Consumers get it pretty quickly because they don't have as much skin in the game, but when you're talking to those whose livelihood is affected by these decisions it can be a harder sell," said Biel. "But having sustainability as a part of our story has been incredible. And it's been great for our company on many levels. We were featured in *Forbes*, for example, because of our sustainability initiatives.

Now, onto the Legend of Ghost Hill and the burying of the bourbon. In 2017, some of the fellas from the distillery team had rented a backhoe for the day, and they wound up with some free time. "One of the boys said 'Hey! I've got an idea! Ghost Hill Ranch? Let's bury some barrels!'" said Biel. They wanted to take a few barrels and bury them to be resurrected at a later date in order to see what the difference would be between a buried barrel and one in the rickhouse. So they built some caskets out of pallets, said a whole eulogy for the bourbon, poured whiskey over the dirt, and voila! "One of the distillers had used a black spray paint can to mark on the fence where the bourbon was buried. We, completely by chance, pulled up the Ghost Hill barrel. Sheer luck. So when I found it, I was like 'Where's the companion barrel?' and they were like 'What are you talking about?' So I started digging into all of these records to figure out which of these barrels had been filled on the same day and thankfully, there was one left." The plan was to pull the barrel out of the ground on Harvest Day, but Biel convinced everyone to pull it out a couple weeks early in order to, you know, make sure that the barrel hadn't shattered and also make sure whatever was in there was drinkable. The barrel was intact and Harvest Day went off without a hitch. They buried six barrels in their coffins. Three of the barrels are distilled beers they make and one is distilled beer from Real Ale. The last barrel is a *starka*, a traditional Polish spirit, which is essentially a barrel-aged vodka.

Treaty Oak is also sitting on a single barrel made from the wood of two fallen Post Oak trees. Since Post Oak is a native Texas tree and oak is the requirement for aging bourbon, they're going to have, to knowledge, the only bourbon whiskey to ever be aged in Post Oak. Their cooper, Kelvin Cooperage, took all of the staves they sent, but only managed to get one barrel out of them. It's not sustainable, but they also didn't cut these trees down to try it out.

The freedom of expression and the creativity at Treaty Oak is palpable. It's pretty incredible to see this level of creativity with an equal dedication to sustainability. There's a discussion that includes the construction of a three-story, climate-controlled rickhouse, in which they would be able to mimic the temperature and humidity levels of Bardstown, Kentucky, or Islay, Scotland, or, more simply, the Texas Gulf Coast or the Panhandle or the West Texas desert. This would not only show the impact on distillate but also compare them directly to a distillate aged in Texas to see what the true impact of the Texas climate is on whiskey.

"We are guided by that space in creativity that allows for maximum output. We are not bound by any convention. We are an amalgam of individuals with varied backgrounds and what we bring to each other are different perspectives and questions. We all have a deep-seated passion for learning and pushing the boundaries. So that, in combination, creates this furnace of creativity," Biel explained. "There's competition in Texas whiskey, resoundingly. But there's also this kinship and this willingness to work together for the common good. If you're making a Texas whiskey, it should say so and if you're buying MGP juice, it should say so. The conversation about quality and transparency is fundamentally important to us and we've found that it also is for our competitors, who are also our allies. We're all in this community and we're mostly advocating for the same things. Knowing that we're all Texans and in it together against the big dogs in Kentucky and Tennessee is pretty special."

GHOST HILL BOURBON

The mash bill is 57% corn, 32% soft red winter wheat, and 11% barley with a minimum age of 18 months, but it doesn't taste young.

PROOF: 95

NOSE: Chardonnay, papaya, gingerbread pear loaf, smoked oysters.

PALATE: Olive oil, dry with a short finish, hemp, grilled peaches, feels hot for a 95 proof, savory, pipe tobacco, Bing cherries.

DAY DRINKER TEXAS BOURBON

A lower proof, younger version of the Ghost Hill; the intention was to create an approachable "day drinking" option.

PROOF: 80

NOSE: Cream soda, iced sugar cookies, waffles with butter and maple syrup, Honey Nut Cheerios.

PALATE: Light mouthfeel, state fair caramel corn, honeysuckle, ground nutmeg, buttered grits.

CERTIFIED TEXAS WHISKEY

TREATY OAK

THE

DAY DRINKER
TEXAS BOURBON

BOURBON WHISKEY
AGED AT LEAST 12 MONTHS

750ML   ALC. 40% BY VOL.   (80 PROOF)

RED, WHITE & BLUE BOURBON WHISKEY

This was a special, distillery-only release for the Fourth of July; the mash bill is the same as the Ghost Hill, but the yellow dent corn was replaced with a combination of heirloom Hopi blue corn and white corn. This is a single barrel that has been aged for 28 months.

PROOF: 95

NOSE: Vanilla crème anglaise, young coconut water, hominy, cinnamon bark, dryer sheets.

PALATE: Oily, moist firewood, guajillo chile, young leather, clover honey, panna cotta, sandalwood, slightly fennel on the fairly short finish.

BOTTLED OLD FASHIONED

What in Sam Hill? Look...I know...but why? Because it's fantastic. This is absolutely the best bottled cocktail in Texas, no matter what fake Ranch Water people are trying to tell you. It's well balanced, it's simple, and if you throw it on the rocks you have a great cocktail, but if you keep it neat it's almost like a super, super sweet whiskey, probably because the damn thing is 75 proof. It's not sickly sweet, it's nice and stout, and it's the best of this style product I've had. Knocks Slow & Low out of the water.

 PROOF: 76

NOSE: Sweetened bourbon with a hint of aromatic bitters.

PALATE: Luckily, it tastes like an Old Fashioned.

BEAT THE TEXAS HEAT!

Justin Ware was named Heaven Hill's Bartender of the Year in 2019, and this drink is everything you want on a hot day in Texas. Taking inspiration from drinking sweet peach tea while sitting on the front porch, it is light, refreshing, and easy to sip in the sweltering summer sun.

2 oz. Treaty Oak Ghost Hill Bourbon

½ oz. peach liqueur

4 dashes Bittermens Orange Cream Citrate

1 pinch salt (optional)

4 oz. Topo Chico, to top

1 strip of lemon peel

1. Combine all of the ingredients, except the Topo Chico, in a highball glass, stir gently, and top with ice. Add the Topo Chico, express lemon peel over the drink, and garnish with the expressed peel and mint.

GULF COAST ★

GULF COAST

FOR YEARS, HOUSTON HAS BEEN KNOWN as one of the most diverse cities in the US. Being the heart of the Gulf Region, Houston's crazy humidity, unfortunate attraction of hurricanes, and general proximity to an ocean, make for entirely different obstacles when it comes to making whiskey. The Gulf Coast is an incredibly unique place, with incredibly unique whiskey coming out of it, which is as diverse as the area itself. Make sure you read "Texas is in. That's the Tweet," to hear more about the impact of the Houston market on the whiskey industry (see page 468). It's genuinely shocking and amazing. Keep an eye on this region. Without hyperbole, there are some innovators here that have the opportunity to change the whiskey industry.

GULF COAST DISTILLERS

SADLY, IN TEXAS YOU'LL NEVER HEAR about a distillery that was started in the 1820s, buried in a cavern during the Civil War, and rediscovered only after the ghost of a distillery cat found someone's great-great-great grandfather's mash bill with a treasure map on the back. What a shame. Our origin stories are usually rooted in entrepreneurship, not fabricated legends.

The origin of Gulf Coast Distillers, however, does reach back to the 1920s. Carlos de Aldecoa Fernandez started his coffee business in Madrid. When the Spanish Civil War forced the family to flee the country, they took their enterprise to Veracruz, Mexico. In 1963, his son, Carlos de Aldecoa Pereda, took over the family business and in 1985 moved their operation to Houston, where they have been ever since.

Today, Carlos de Aldecoa Bueno oversees his family's businesses. I'm not sure if I can properly convey the sheer size and level of influence this family has in the US coffee industry. Eximius Coffee is roasting and ground packaging, so they do private label and contract manufacturing for other companies like Maxwell House or a major retailer like HEB in addition to the retail brands they also own, like Cappio, Aldecoa, Café Diario, and several other brands. They also own Cadeco Industries, which is a warehousing and distribution company that owns about 1.5 million-square-feet of space, primarily for green coffee storage. "We touch, in some capacity, between 30% and 40% of the coffee that is consumed in the United States." Read that again. Yes, at least one-third of the coffee in the US runs through this family, according to de Aldecoa Bueno. The only way to truly understand the scope of this is to visit.

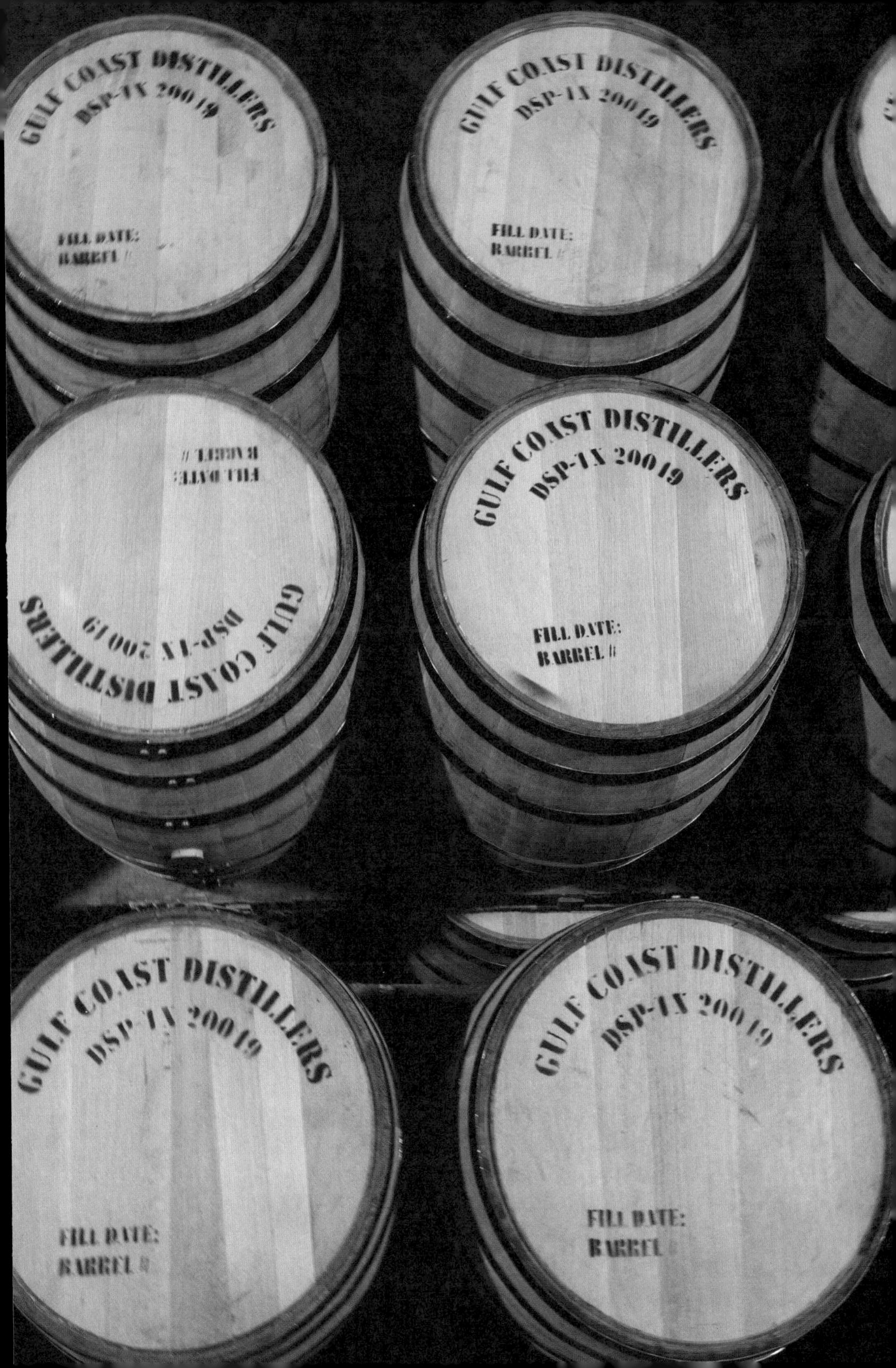
GULF COAST DISTILLERS
DSP-TX 20019
FILL DATE:
BARREL #

"We bought this building probably twenty-five years ago from Uncle Ben's Rice. When I graduated from engineering school, I wanted to build my own place. I thought I could take this old rice plant and convert it into a coffee manufacturing plant. I borrowed the money from my father and he said that I had twelve months to pay him back or he would become a partner. I was not interested in having any partners so I did my very best to quickly get the business up and running to pay him back," de Aldecoa Bueno explained with a laugh. "This building was built in the 1930s by the US Department of Defense. All of the rice used in World War II came out of this plant. So the legacy and history of this facility is pretty great and today we've converted into a distillery, but we're still making an agricultural product and it's been a great journey."

As the owner and founder of Gulf Coast Distillers, de Aldecoa Bueno oversees the most impressive distillery in Texas when you're talking about sheer magnitude and scope of production. Frankly, once they have finalized their expansion, they will be the largest distillery west of the Mississippi. Gulf Coast Distillers, within five years, will be one of the most important, influential distillers on the planet. Full freakin' stop.

The decision to enter into the spirits industry was based in the relationships that de Aldecoa Bueno already had on the coffee side. His family's companies have been entrenched in the retail side of the coffee industry, so when they looked at the spirits market and particular barriers of entry in the Texas three-tier system, he decided to come at it from a multi-brand and multi-product angle. They had an opportunity to approach retailers with all but absolute certainty that they would be able to fulfill any orders and grow exponentially, which is a major problem among craft distillers. Scale is probably the largest single struggle for a craft distiller once they've found their distributor and found the retail partners that support them. Think about it like a restaurant. If your favorite dish was only available every fourth time you wanted to order it, eventually, you might decide it's not worth the hassle and you'd no longer order it.

Here's the kicker. Gulf Coast Distillers is 100% Texas grain to glass. They are responsible for keeping thousands of acres of farms in business, and keeping a massive amount of production dollars in Texas. They are providing brands an opportunity to have a truly Texas whiskey, from the growing of the corn to the bottling line, at an unmatched scale. Once you are dealing with the scale of products that they are, 6 to 7 million gallons of spirits a year, the typical company doesn't choose the more expensive route in order to support the local economy. This is, easily, the most impressive part of the company and we, as Texans, are implausibly lucky that de Aldecoa Bueno can commit this magnitude of resources.

One of the most important elements of the Gulf Coast business model is the continuation of the private label approach in which they have been excelling at for years on the coffee end. They're currently making private label spirits for multiple companies and giving others the opportunity to compete in the Texas whiskey market. Now, this makes it a little more complicated for me to tell you all about which whiskeys are "really" from Texas, but it's also going to cause the global spirits industry to become acutely aware of our little start-up whiskey industry.

One of the biggest names in the industry was hired to help turn the coffee factory into a massive distillery. "I've always liked creating a process and learning how to retool equipment and I think that's what attracted Dave Pickerell to us," de Aldecoa Bueno explained. "Instead of buying a new Vendome still, my process was focused on rebuilding this industrial complex and his engineering background and my engineering background were a great fit." Pickerell helped build the equipment, helped establish the processes, helped set the mash bills, and helped set this distillery out on the right foot from the beginning.

Being on the Gulf Coast has proved to present some incredibly unique issues. "We're aging Texas whiskey at sea-level. In some cases the proof will only go up one percent," said Julian Giraldo, the head distiller at Gulf Coast, who used to oversee the coffee operations before diving head first into whiskey. "We're playing with all sorts of different entry proof because of this. We're doing dozens of experiments." They have different barrels, different grains, different yeast strains, different distillates. (One of the coolest things I tasted was a brandy they're still sitting on.) "I'm grateful to have had Dave Pickerell as a mentor on the distilling end, but I'm also grateful to come from a coffee background because both coffee and whiskey come from grain and have specific attractive flavor profiles. I had to learn how to taste and produce coffee a long time ago."

"One of the projects that we were working on with Dave was a Canadian rye that would be aged or finished in a bourbon barrel in Texas. We brought in some tankers from Alberta, we have some 9- and some 12-year-old product that we are finishing in our barrels. Some of it is finishing in our wheated bourbon barrels and some is finishing in our rye barrels. We're going to be releasing it under a new trademarked brand called 'Pickerell' to honor his family," said de Aldecoa Bueno.

"It was something that we wanted to do after he passed. He was instrumental in helping us understand large-scale and quality production of whiskey. It's unfortunate that he passed, but we are still connected with his family and wanted to help support them."

Gulf Coast Distillers was also single-handedly responsible for the creation and distribution of over 100,000 gallons of hand sanitizer in the Houston area during the time of COVID-19. They also helped other Texas distilleries turn hand sanitizer into a temporary revenue source, which, no doubt, kept dozens of small businesses open when facing monumental odds. "We take the idea of being a good neighbor very seriously," said Carlos de Aldecoa Bueno.

One day, Gulf Coast Distillers will be producing at the same rate as Sazarac or Dickel or MGP, but it will still be 100% Texas born and raised whiskey. Their importance cannot be understated. Full freakin' stop.

GIANT 95 BOURBON

This flagship bourbon is much more stout than its 91-proof little brother; it's Texas from grain to glass.

PROOF: 95

NOSE: Smells young, butterscotch pie, grain heavy, guaiacol with a smoky nuance.

PALATE: Vanilla extract, dark chocolate bread pudding, toasted oak, green tobacco.

GIANT 100 STRAIGHT RYE

Gulf Coast's new rye expression is a Certified Texas Whiskey.

PROOF: 100

NOSE: Cinnamon-sugar bagel, rye grain, dried apricot, Red Hot candies.

PALATE: Dry, grips the tongue, freshly cracked black pepper, vanilla cream puff, salted caramel apple pie, new cowhide.

MKT DISTILLERY

IN THE LATE 1800S, Texas had a major transportation problem. The settlements in the state were primarily confined to the river bottoms in East and South Texas and along the Gulf Coast. Texas rivers have never been deep enough for year-round transportation, so enter Texas' savior, the railroad. The rapid increase in construction of railroads began in the 1850s and by the 1870s the railroads had become the most powerful industrial force in the state.

The MKT Railroad (Missour–Kansas–Texas) was the first railroad to enter Texas from the north. The nickname for the railroad was KT or Katy. Was that a light bulb that just turned on? Yes, you're correct. If you're in or from Texas, whatever "Katy" you're thinking about, be it the city near Houston, the trail that runs through Dallas, or the state park, all are remnants of the MKT Railroad.

Today, you can still see sections of the MKT across Texas, but, of course, my favorite place to do so is about thirty feet outside the MKT Distillery in the town named after the railroad. When Nick and Nici Jessett started their distillery, they wanted to embrace the area's legacy, so they started with the railroad and they ended with rice. The greater Katy area was the rice capital of the South. During its heyday, there were over 70,000 acres of rice in production in these parts. Enormous rice silos have become a symbol of the area's heritage, which is why the Jessetts have chosen to place their operation amongst these giants.

The key differentiator for MKT Distillery is their use of rice in their mash bills. Upward of 20% of their whiskey is made with rice, a very deliberate decision to honor their community. "When people try our white whiskey, they always comment that it's a calmer flavor profile than they were expecting," Nick says. "You have to remember that a lot of light beers are made with rice and so it makes sense that the rice mellows it out."

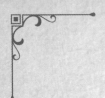
Driving up to the distillery, along the old MKT Railroad tracks, you can't quite tell how large the Katy rice silos are until you get close. The distillery itself is inside the factory and, obviously, it feels industrial but somehow also feels like a neighborhood pub. It actually reminds me of one of those back patios in New Orleans, buried in concrete, but beautiful and open at the same time. MKT is the little distillery around the corner that happens to be inside a massive, historically significant industrial marvel. If you're a cigar fan, you can literally stand inside the silos and enjoy their cigar lounge. The vibe is hyper-local and it couldn't be more obvious that these spirits are made by and for the people of Katy.

CONDUCTOR'S RESERVE

The first in the new "Heritage" series, this has a mash bill of corn, barley, and rice; all grains are Texas grown and the rice is grown in Katy. Proof varies.

PROOF: 95

NOSE: Fresh bell pepper, forest floor, limoncello, confectioners' sugar, raked leaves, very light.

PALATE: Oily, light up front, heavy in the tail, fresh lumber, cabbage, cork, buttermilk, chile negro, roasted corn on the cob.

OLD HUMBLE DISTILLING COMPANY

THERE ARE MANY WAYS TO DESCRIBE JOSEPH BREDA, owner of Old Humble Distilling Company, but humble isn't one of them. Breda consistently brags about his whiskey like a deservedly proud papa. "In your hand, you have the gold medal winning... the only gold medal winning whiskey from the 2020 London International Spirits competition... The highest ranked American whiskey... The only whiskey to beat my Straight Whiskey," he told me on my visit to his new distillery.

Originally Big Thicket Distilling, Breda bought out his original partners, changed the name, and moved the operation from Conroe to Humble. When he was asked to produce a substantial amount of whiskey by a large chain liquor store, Breda found that the best way to meet the demand was to source a portion of the juice from outside of Texas. Thus, his Old Humble Straight Whiskey is "born in the hills of Kentucky and finished in the oilfield of Humble." Ultimately, the plan is to be making 100% of their products with all Texas ingredients. He's also planning on moving into different grained whiskeys, including a rice whiskey that will pay homage to the predominate Gulf Coast grain.

"I don't want to make a whiskey that you have to fight your way to the bottom of the glass," Breda said. "I don't want to make a whiskey where the bottle lasts six years. I want to make a whiskey that you want to share with your friends. I have no interest in making hard-to-drink, heavy, overbearing shlock that you've convinced yourself is good because you paid $300 for the bottle. The type of whiskey I aspire to make is the type of whiskey that you accidentally run out of while watching a baseball game. It's a recreational drug for crying out loud. You shouldn't be fighting when you drink it."

Old Humble is a dichotomy. It is the blood, sweat, and tears of a Texan with a massive personality, who happens to be making light, delicate, easy-drinking whiskey.

"I like to call it whiskey the way whiskey should taste. A lot of the new bourbon makers are going the way the craft brewers did where they were just hopping the shit out of their IPAs and they're pounding them and pounding them with overbearing flavors and it's like chewing on tobacco leaves. That's not my thing. Life is too short for bad bourbon and too long to do nothing about it."

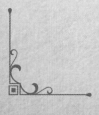

STRAIGHT WHISKEY

This is a sourced whiskey with a mash bill of 91% corn and 9% barley, aged 5 in used bourbon barrels.

PROOF: 90

NOSE: Brown sugar butter, menthol, agave syrup, honey roasted almonds.

PALATE: Sweet creamed corn, cinnamon and sugar, pencil rubber, sugar cream pie.

SPECIAL RESERVE

This is the Straight Whiskey re-barreled in a new 5-gallon barrel for an additional 3 months.

PROOF: 90

NOSE: Rice pudding, vanilla wafer cookies, candied almonds.

PALATE: Oily, anise but still light, vanilla cream, caramel apples.

SHIRE DISTILLING

IT'S AN INCREDIBLY AMERICAN STORY when a family collectively decides to go into distilling. Practically every major distiller in Kentucky comes from a family legacy of some sort. It's been fantastic to see these truly family-run distilleries flourishing in Texas. Shire Distilling is the embodiment of family distilling.

In 2015, Tim Raines started trying to piece together the parts to build a still when he saw an ad for an entire distillery being for sale. He forwarded the email to his dad, George Daher, and the next day they went to give it a look. They didn't buy that distillery, but the seed had been planted.

Both Daher and Raines come from homebrew backgrounds, but once the decision was made, they both headed out to Virginia for two weeks to learn the craft of distillation, and Shire Distilling received their distillers permit in 2017. Like many other start-up distillers, they were producing their own distillate on a small scale but sourcing some products in order to keep the lights on. They are currently working toward making 100% of their products. One of the interesting techniques that Shire is using is the addition of barrel staves to their barrels to enhance the interaction between the wood and the whiskey. And while they may have started distilling on a 50-gallon baby still, they have since built out a semi-automated, process-controlled distillery with a capacity of 600 gallons.

One of the most interesting expressions is their Shire Centaur, made from a No Label Brewery Milk Stout they had aged in a used bourbon barrel that went sour. They were able to distill exactly one barrel's worth and it was aged for two years and three months before release. This was some of the very first distillate that Shire made on their original 50-gallon baby still.

SHIRE CENTAUR

Made from only enough No Label Brewery Milk Stout to age for 27 months in a single new American oak barrel.

PROOF: 100.2

NOSE: Hint of locker room, honey, figs, cheesy and yeasty.

PALATE: Chocolate malt, cinnamon, crushed red pepper, espresso you let cool off for too long.

SHIRE OAK

A sourced young whiskey, somewhere between 6 months and a year, with a mash bill of 75% corn, 21% rye, and 4% barley.

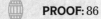 **PROOF:** 86

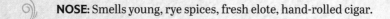 **NOSE:** Smells young, rye spices, fresh elote, hand-rolled cigar.

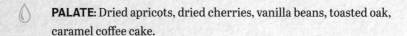 **PALATE:** Dried apricots, dried cherries, vanilla beans, toasted oak, caramel coffee cake.

WHITMEYER'S DISTILLING CO.

SHORTLY AFTER 9/11, Travis and Chris Whitmeyer enlisted together in the US Army. After completing basic training, they wound up being stationed in Germany. "When I was in Germany, I started dating one of the local girls. She invited me over for supper one evening and being a good diplomat, I brought them some Hershey's chocolate and a case of Budweiser. They loved the chocolate and hated the beer," Travis told me. Turns out that the German family's farm had been turning crops into various beers, wines, and schnapps for generations. "Her grandfather made all of this beer and schnapps and we'd sneak down into the basement and grab a bottle of this or that and man, some of these could have been a hundred years old for all we knew!" Travis fell in love with the whole idea of making distilled products and had a specific hankering for whiskey.

Once their tours were done, both brothers moved to Houston to go to school. "One of my first business classes, I had to write a business plan, so I wrote one for a distillery," Travis told me. He was able to talk his brother and his father, Wesley, into helping him start the business, which, to this day, is still entirely family owned and operated. The Whitmeyer family has now been in Texas for seven generations.

One of the more interesting obstacles that Whitmeyer's had to tackle is the simple process of aging. This part of whiskey making in Texas is... How do I put this? Chaos. Stuart Brown, Whitmeyer's head distiller, told me that there have been barrels that have lost alcohol and water at the same rate. "We even had a couple that lost alcohol at a faster rate than water because of the humidity down here. We were literally losing proof as it aged. It was wild," Brown said. The various environments in Texas will always create a unique set of circumstances that distillers have to deal with as their product ages. The Gulf Coast is going to be very different from Hill Country or North Texas.

"We do a little bit of everything. We certainly distill our own but our permit allows us to do all sorts of things with spirits and I don't want to limit us by saying we're never going to do this or that. We have Kentucky distillate that we age here. We're also sourcing some MGP rye," said Travis. This methodology has led them to creating the only bourbon-rye blend that I've seen in Texas.

Whitmeyer's is another family-run operation that is building their own legacy right now. "My mentality from day one has been to keep it simple. I definitely applaud those in our industry that have put so much energy into using these different grains and finishes but we're just trying to be straightforward," Travis told me. "Five years ago, Texas had a really, really bad rep on a national level. It's been great to see the shift and, sure, you'll see holdouts, but the argument that the only decent whiskey in American is from Kentucky is dwindling. Rapidly." Couldn't agree more, my man.

BOURBON & RYE

A blend of bourbon distilled in Texas and Kentucky and a rye distilled in Indiana; each bottle is a slightly different blend. If you happen to end up with a batch number with a "C" at the beginning of it, that is a single barrel; some blends were batched and bottled and others were re-barreled in new charred oak barrels. One dollar of every bottle sold goes to Camp Hope, a foundation supporting veterans with PTSD.

 **PROOF:** 108

NOSE: Cherry Lifesaver, spice raisin jam, vanilla marscapone, roasted quince.

PALATE: Raspberry truffle cake, maple bacon, extinguished campfire, Vegemite, sweet on the front, slightly bitter fennel on the finish.

TEXAS SINGLE BARREL
CASK STRENGTH

Sourced 5- to 7-year-old whiskey that is aged in their barrel warehouse and bottled at cask strength, which will be varied; the type of whiskey you'd like to sip while enjoying a good cigar.

PROOF: 112

NOSE: Lemon zest, vanilla bean, caramel, charred oak, dried cherries, dried blueberries.

PALATE: Smoked cedar plank, citrus pith, slight seaweed, wet cardboard, boiled pork, vanilla pound cake.

WHITMEYER'S
— TEXAS —
SINGLE BARREL
CASK STRENGTH

Straight Bourbon Whiskey

— 750 mL —

56% Alc./Vol. (112 Proof)

YELLOW ROSE
DISTILLING

TEXAS HISTORY IS FULL OF FANTASTIC STORIES about those who helped Texas become a republic. As a native Texan, I can honestly say that quite a few of those stories are utter hogwash. Regardless, as the story goes, in 1836 at the Battle of San Jacinto, the Yellow Rose of Texas ensured General Sam Houston's victory and with that became a Texas legend. The Houston distillery named in her honor is working to achieve that same level of notoriety.

Yellow Rose Distilling was founded in 2010 by neighbors Troy Smith and Ryan Baird. After backyard discussions over whiskey morphed into a business plan, Baird convinced Randy Whitaker to join and Yellow Rose launched Outlaw Bourbon Whiskey in July 2012. They also love to tout being the first legal distillery and tasting room in the Houston city limits. In 2017, Spanish wine and spirits firm Zamora Company acquired an equity stake in Yellow Rose. With that, while also ramping up distribution across the US, they've also entered several countries across Europe. Texas is an international brand in and of itself, so the increasing popularity and demand for Texas whiskey across the pond is an opportunity multiple European companies have jumped on. Peck around on YouTube and you'll find an oddly substantial amount of reviews of their whiskey in German.

Yellowrose's head distiller, Houston Farris, has his own familial relationship with the spirits world: "My great-grandfather, Vance Raimond, ran the first legal moonshine still in the state of Texas since Prohibition. This was at the Texas Centennial Expo in 1936. He set up on the midway of the state fairgrounds and attracted a great deal of attention. Unfortunately, that included the IRS, which wasted little time in shutting down his operation." Apparently, we've had a hearty amount of governmental interference in our booze making around these parts for a very long time.

Yellow Rose takes great pride in their 100% grain-to glass-whiskeys, including their Outlaw Bourbon, the Single Malt, and Harris County Bourbon. They are one of the first whiskey makers in Texas and they've been making Outlaw from day one, when they were on a little 40-gallon still. "We want to treat our grain with respect. We're very careful with the cooking process and we're aiming for every mash to be the same yield with the same flavor profile. We'd like to eventually be 100% grain to glass for every single one of our expressions and we've been making strides in that direction for years," said Farris. "We also use a simple pot still distillation because we want as much flavor as possible coming from our mash."

Yellow Rose is also starting to dive into some intense experimentation: different finishing barrels, different fill proofs (the ABV going into the barrel), different sized barrels, different mash bills, and different toast levels. They are an awesome example of the importance of creativity in the Texas whiskey industry.

OUTLAW BOURBON

The 100% grain-to-glass flagship whiskey is a pot-distilled bourbon made from 100% yellow corn and aged in small American oak barrels; originally aged in 3-gallon barrels, but don't freak out, it's in 30- and 53-gallon barrels now.

PROOF: 92

NOSE: Sweet, the crunchy part of a crème brûlée, caramel corn, dark cherry.

PALATE: Butterscotch, very corn forward, buttery, smells like an elote cart.

RYE WHISKEY

This sourced 95% rye, 5% malted barley blend has a stated age of at least a year, but drinks much older.

PROOF: 90

NOSE: Mild vanilla with a touch of cooling piney woodiness, herbal mint tea, light banana.

PALATE: Very light pepper spice, green apple, pennyroyal mint tea.

SINGLE MALT

Double-pot distilled, made with 100% malted Golden Promise barley; surprisingly easy drinking, but grain-forward.

PROOF: 80

NOSE: Raisins, cherry compote, black pepper, roasted pecans.

PALATE: Fruitcake, prunes, viscous, almond toffee, fresh-brewed coffee with a hint of Red Hots.

HARRIS COUNTY BOURBON

New high-rye bourbon with more of a traditional bourbon mash bill than Outlaw; 65% yellow corn, 25% rye, 10% malted barley, all from Texas, aged for at least 2 years. This came out of a series of experiments with 13 unique mash bills and this was the winner-winner chicken dinner.

PROOF: 106

NOSE: Sour cream coffee cake, almond brittle, corn bread, vanilla bean.

PALATE: Spicy, roasted corn, buttery, big mouthfeel, toasted oak, iced sugar cookies.

33 TIMES & NEVER A MISS

After eight years of slinging drinks at some of Houston's most popular haunts, Lacy Williams was approached with the opportunity to launch her first concept. Sixes and Sevens, the colloquial phrase that refers to a state of chaos fits her, and her beautiful bar, to a tee. Just like John Wayne in *McClintock!* this drink never misses. Creamy and boozy, the bold savory caramel hints to sipping this around the campfire under the stars. Smells of crackling bacon and sweet onions, and the round bright Outlaw Bourbon.

1½ oz. Yellow Rose Outlaw Bourbon

½ oz. ruby port

1 oz. Whiskey, Caramelized Onion, and Bacon Caramel

1 egg

1. Combine all of the ingredients in a cocktail shaker and dry shake vigorously.

2. Add ice, shake again, until creamy, and double strain into a chilled glass.

3. Garnish with freshly ground nutmeg and a piece of crispy bacon.

Whiskey, Caramelized Onion, and Bacon Caramel: Chop ½ Vidalia onion and add it to a saucepan over medium-high heat and sweat it for a few minutes before adding 2 tablespoons salted butter. Cook until the onion begins to brown and then deglaze pan with 3 oz. bourbon. Using a slotted spoon, remove the onion and reserve for another use; keep any remaining liquid warm in the pan. Add 1½ cups sugar to a second saucepan over medium heat and melt, stirring constantly. Once melted, add 3 tablespoons room temperature salted butter, 1 tablespoon rendered bacon fat, and the onion liquid from the other pan. Stir until butter and bacon fat melt then slowly stir in ½ cup room temperature heavy cream and allow to boil for 1 minute before removing from heat. Let cool before using.

TEXAS IS IN. THAT'S THE TWEET.

When I made the decision to go to the University of Texas to get my Master's in Emerging Media and Communications, I did so because I figured that, if nothing else, the internet wasn't exactly going anywhere and I might as well try to understand it as well as I possibly could. The power of the internet is absolutely unavoidable and will be so until humans literally decide to turn it off. When you look at something like whiskey, on the surface it may seem like the impact is minimal, but that couldn't be further from the truth.

Texas, and all of the things happening here, have a vital place in the story of whiskey and the internet and while I'll do my best to convey it, if you think I missed something, Google it. "Let me give you an example... I was trying to promote our Facebook group and it felt like an uphill battle, so I started releasing the hard numbers of the revenue the group was responsible for," said Kris Hart, one of the moderators of the Houston Bourbon Society Facebook Group, and the host of Whiskey Neat, the only whiskey-focused terrestrial radio show in Texas. "Last year [2019], HBS did $639,000 in revenue and just shy of 10,000 bottle sales. If we were a bar, that would equate to a $3.5 million bar, except we have no overhead."

The DFW Whiskey Club is one of the original whiskey-oriented Facebook groups; founded in late 2016 it has executed over fifty single barrel picks since. Raymond Taylor, one of the founders said that their club pretty quickly became a vehicle for philanthropy. "We've now been at the forefront of the whiskey community with charitable contributions and donations to support our local community in need. We raised over $70,000 in the first nine months of 2020."

Someone Say Whiskey began as a neighborhood Facebook group less than two years ago, but admin Randal Sullivan told me the group is now "a nationwide group with over 5,000 members and we average a weekly single barrel whiskey."

These are massively influential. Taylor told me DFW Whiskey Club recently "had a distillery change their latest rye release from 100 proof to cask strength, even after the initial TTB approval, due to our recommendations and support of their product." These groups are legitimately doing things that no one else is. They're importing spirits directly into the state, they're able to get offerings that just don't exist without their influence. "The three largest spirits markets in the US are New York, California, and Texas and we are doing things in this state that are not happening anywhere else. We're getting full state distribution for certain spirits because of our Facebook groups that wouldn't have happened otherwise. If you're writing about what's happening in Texas, above and beyond Texas whiskey, just the simple fact that the excitement and the camaraderie of these groups that have been put together in Texas are driving this industry. I mean, now's the time to write the book for sure, because literally anything is possible," Hart told me.

The Houston Bourbon Society is certainly the big dog of the bunch. They're doing things on a scale that no one else in America is doing. They are a major part of the reason that the single largest spirits market in North America is Houston. Hart said, "Between the impact of our Facebook groups and our YouTube channels, and the only radio show about spirits and some of the best festivals in the US, there couldn't be a better place to be a whiskey fan right now than Texas." Speaking of YouTube, y'all know the Whiskey Tribe, the most popular whiskey channel on YouTube, is from Texas, yeah? If not, see page 285. They have almost 400,000 followers on one channel and over 250,000 on the other one...and that one is only marginally about whiskey. Kidding, but also not kidding. Also, the Texas Whiskey Association has an incredible YouTube channel with some superb interviews with their members, who also happen to be some of the best whiskey makers in the state. I highly recommend subscribing to that one.

I'd also be remiss if I didn't mention some of the incredible podcasts coming out of Texas. I remember talking to Mike G, the host of Show deVie after my first book and he was telling me about how his intention was simply to document this explosion of spirits and spirits culture and his podcast has some of the best interviews I've heard with some incredible industry juggernauts. Sullivan from

Someone Say Whiskey also hosts a show called Bourbon Real Talk, and has a bit of a focus on Texas whiskey as of late, so you'll be able to find some interesting discussions about your favorite Texas whiskeys there. Whiskey Neat, the radio show is also a YouTube show and a podcast, in case you are not in the greater Houston area and would like to listen. I'd also like to give a special shout out to Wade Woodard and his blog Tater-Talk. If you have any particular interest in hardcore legal classifications of whiskey-related laws or a barrage of information about those in violation of TTB labeling code, Woodward is your guy.

How does this relate to Texas whiskey, you ask? It's remarkable that we're able to get the kind of traction on the kinds of projects the state has become interested in because of these online groups. But, more importantly, this is a key driver of innovation. The innovative ways the groups have been able to operate within the restrictions of the TABC laws have made our distillers more creative. Sullivan told me Someone Say Whiskey was working on some barrel picks that were, essentially, going to be distributed by the distilleries themselves on site, so it allows the distillery to make a larger margin on those bottles, which is incredibly important during, oh, let's see, a pandemic. I was invited to Balcones with the HBS crew for their latest round of barrel picks and essentially watched them shop for whiskey and rum barrels like anyone else would for vinyl at Record Store Day. The Whiskey Tribe guys helped distribute their collaboration whiskey they made with the Texas Whiskey Festival through their Patreon and Facebook groups.

Hart ended with this, which, somehow, is exactly what I needed to hear to put my feeling about this industry into words. I knew there was something inherently special about our whiskey makers here, but Hart boiled it down: "The one thing Texas has done differently, is they've said yes." He went on to explain how if you were to "go to Heaven Hill and say 'we'd like to do a barrel proof...' they'll say 'No, we don't do that.' You go to Maker's Mark and say we want to do a ten-year Maker's Mark, 'No, we don't do that.' Everything is a 'no' out of Kentucky because they are so massive that these little individual barrel projects do not seem worth it to them. But everyone in Texas has said 'Yes, let's do it.' We emptied a barrel of Elijah Craig and we took it to a local honey bee farmer and he aged honey in it for three months. And then we took that barrel, with about five gallons of honey left in it, and we went to Balcones and said 'Hey! We want to put your single malt in there.' And the answer is yes. And, in my opinion, the explosive growth in the Texas whiskey industry is because they are willing to entertain us, and they choose to be a part of the social media world, and then, like any good Texan, they go above and beyond. You want something cool? They say let's do something cool." That's not happening anywhere else.

The Whiskey Tribe, Houston Bourbon Society, DFW Whiskey Club, Someone Say Whiskey, Liquor Hound, Whiskey Crusaders, the Dallas Scotch Society, Texas Whiskey Consortium, East Texas Bourbon Society, Austin Bourbon Club—I could just…keep…going. The clout that our state has developed in the spirits world is truly mind-blowing, and here's the best part of all of this – it's free. This is the beauty of the internet. Information is free. Community is free. If you'd like to find yourself a home amongst whiskey groups, I'll invite you to join any of those mentioned above. Also, since we're talking internet, if you'd like additional information or links to any of these groups, go to texaswhiskeybook.com where you'll find a thousand things I wanted to include in this, but wasn't able to. Maybe I'll even start a Facebook group.

GRUB, GEAR, AND GOOD TIMES ★

Grub, Gear, and Good Times

THERE'S MORE TO TEXAS THAN WHISKEY. I know you know that, but I know a thing or two about these things, so here are spots I highly recommend as you tour the state sipping our whiskey wares.

NORTH TEXAS

LAS ALMAS ROTAS

3615 Parry Ave., Dallas, TX 75226

When you've had enough whiskey, but you're not quite done drinking, it's mezcal time, y'all. Las Almas Rotas is irreproachably the perfect Texas mezcaleria. They have a deftly curated spirits selection and the knowledge to tell you about all of it. There is no Texas whiskey here, but try theirincredible special edition Gracias a Dios Pechuga de Brisket, made with Texas smoked brisket.

REVOLVER TAQUERIA

2701 Main St., #120, Dallas, TX 75226

This is the best taqueria I've ever been to, and I'm half Mexican, and possibly more opinionated about tacos than I am about whiskey. Revolver is a taqueria in Deep Ellum in Dallas and if you're nearby, you'll want to swing by. Working off family recipes, Chef Regino Rojas is an absolute culinary giant and deserves a Nobel Peace Prize for his Pulpo Taco. What? It's science.

DALLAS FARMERS MARKET

920 S Harwood St., Dallas, TX 75201

One of the highlights of many a weekend, this is home to artisan culinary treats of all sorts. It's an overwhelming sensory experience as you stroll around, buying the freshest produce from local farmers. If the lines are too long, head over to Ka-Tip's storefront for some of the most authentic and delicious Thai food in Texas.

FORT WORTH ZOO

1989 Colonial Pkwy., Fort Worth, TX 76110

I grew up going here once a year in elementary school and man, I miss it. There's a reason it was voted the best zoo in the US. It's a wonderland and the perfect way to spend a Texas fall afternoon. Fun fact: it was founded in 1909 with one lion, two bear cubs, an alligator, a coyote, a peacock, and a few rabbits.

HEIM BBQ

1109 W Magnolia Ave., Fort Worth, TX 76104

When Daniel Vaughn, the BBQ Editor for *Texas Monthly*, says, "Heim BBQ is the current gold standard of Fort Worth Barbeque," you should trust him. The pork belly burnt ends are a culinary wonder and must be respected. Bonus, they have the best burger you'll ever have too. Seriously. Bigger bonus, they might just have the best whiskey selection in Fort Worth.

BARS

THE USUAL
1408 W Magnolia Ave., Fort Worth, TX 76104

Founded by the godfather of Fort Worth cocktails, Brad Hensarling, The Usual
is one of the best cocktail bars in the country. Dark, cozy, with unbelievable
cocktails thanks to the current team running the show, led by head bartender
Jason Pollard.

THE CELT
100 N Tennessee St., McKinney, TX 75069
Winner of North American Irish Pub of the Year in 2019, this little gem is a blast.
The award is cool, but the Irish-style whiskey they have worked with Ironroot to
create is much cooler. It's unlike anything else coming from that distillery and
The Celt is the only place with it.

EAST SIDE
117 E Oak St., Denton, TX 76201

PASCHALL BAR
122 N Locust St. Denton, TX 76201

THE LIBERTINE
2101 Greenville Ave., Dallas, TX 75206

God bless the Libertine. This is the place where many a Dallasite have learned
how to drink and what a proper whiskey is. I can honestly say that my interest in
any of this stuff came from nights at the Libertine and their whiskey and cocktail
programs.

SECOND FLOOR
13340 Dallas Parkway, Dallas, TX 75240

TRINITY HALL
5321 E Mockingbird Lane #250, Dallas, TX 75206

BARREL & BONES

2801 Plano Pkwy., Suite #140, The Colony, TX 75056

Formerly of Fort Worth fame, they have one of the most comprehensive Texas whiskey selections in the state. And some damn fine fried deviled eggs. You're welcome.

STANDARD POUR

2900 McKinney Ave., Dallas, TX 75204

THOMPSON'S

900 Houston St., Fort Worth, TX 76102

JAXON BEER GARDEN

311 S Akard St., Dallas, TX 75202

When AT&T selected Dallas as their home, they bought up four blocks of downtown and have created a paradise inside the city. This is one of the only places in Texas where you can grab a drink and wander. The food hall next door is incredible, with some of the best that Dallas has to offer, but the beer garden is the crown jewel. Amazing selection of Texas whiskey and Texas whiskey-based cocktails created by one of the city's most celebrated barmen, Alex Fletcher.

UNION BEAR

5880 TX State Hwy. 121, Suite 101, Plano, TX 75024

LIQUOR STORES

EIGHTER LIQUOR

1845 S FM-51, Decatur, TX 76234

M&R LIQUOR

5901 Bell St., Suite C7, Amarillo, TX 79109

BAR & GARDEN

3314 Ross Ave., Suite 150, Dallas, TX 75204

Bar & Garden is simply wonderful, with an amazing selection for a boutique store. They host all sorts of tasting events and are incredibly careful in their approach to their inventory. No matter what you end up selecting, it's already been so well curated that you'll love it.

EMPIRE LIQUOR

901 W Spring Creek Pkwy., #145, Plano, TX 75023

MIRAGE FINE SPIRITS

4405 Colleyville Blvd., Suite 110, Colleyville, TX 76034

POGO'S WINE & SPIRITS

5360 West Lovers Lane, Dallas, TX 75209

The premier indie liquor store in Dallas. Pogo's probably has it, regardless of what it is. They carry some of the most unique whiskeys in the area and they've forgotten more about whiskey than most whiskey YouTube reviewers will ever know.

ANGEL'S BEVERAGE CENTER

901 E Plano Pkwy., Suite 109, Plano, TX 75074

LAKEWOOD MEDALLION LIQUOR

5748 Live Oak St., Dallas, TX 75206

LOYALTY LIQUORS

5749 TX-121, The Colony, TX 75056

One of the main places used by local whiskey clubs to facilitate their barrel selections, so randomly you could find some pretty unique stuff. They have a great selection and are incredibly knowledgeable.

BIG COUNTRY LIQUOR BEER & WINE

6619 Forest Hill Dr. # 45, Forest Hill, TX 76140

CENTRAL TEXAS

SLOVACEK'S

214 Melodie Dr., West, TX 76691

I have been saying for thirty years that my favorite food is klobasnek. But no one ever seems to know what that is. It's a sausage and cheese kolache. Now you know. These god-like Czech creations have become a road trip tradition for many a Texan. I was a huge fan of the folks on the north-bound side forever, but as of late, I gotta tell you, the best kolaches in West are those on the south-bound side.

MAGNOLIA MARKET AT THE SILOS

601 Webster Ave., Waco, TX 76706

Chip and Jojo would like to formally invite y'all to Waco. This is where you can buy a variety of expertly curated items that they have carefully slapped their name on. The stars of HGTV's *Fixer Upper* have created a massive influx of tourism for Waco and their renovation of this area is truly stunning. And it's down the street from Balcones, so it's a perfect place to send your non-whiskey drinking better halves.

DICHOTOMY COFFEE & SPIRITS

508 Austin Ave., Waco, TX 76701

This is a modern coffee shop that just happens to have Waco's best cocktails in the back. You'll also be able to find Balcones expressions here that, frankly, cannot be found anywhere else. When I needed to track down a taste of the Balcones Hechiceros and the Brujeria, this is where I was able to do so. They also make an exceptional clarified milk punch.

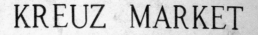

LOCKHART, THE BBQ MECCA

Thirty-five miles southeast of Austin, with a population of 13,000, Lockhart is officially known as the Barbecue Capital of Texas, according to the Texas Legislature. The three spots you need to know are Kreuz Market (get the brisket and pork chop), Smitty's Market (sausage and pork ribs), and Black's Barbecue (beef rib, brisket, and turkey), and you'll probably want to bring a cooler.

BUC EE'S

Across Texas on every interstate highway

You know everything's bigger in Texas right? Well, that includes this massive convenience store chain that you'll run into about every 100 miles or so as you traverse the state. The food's solid (except the kolaches) and it has . . . everything. But don't try the Beaver Nuggets unless you're ready for a new obsession, and to join a gym.

BERDOLL PECAN FARM

2626 State Hwy. 71 West, Cedar Creek, TX 78612

Berdoll has been family owned and operated for thirty-three years. The farm is 340 acres and has 15,000 trees in the orchard and 90,000 in the nursery. This is their retail outlet for all things pecan.

ROHAN'S MEADERY

6002 FM2981, La Grange, TX 78945

Keeping with the traditions of the settlers of the area, these meads are prepared in a Czech style, resulting in a crisp, clean, and slightly drier end product. Located on Blissful Folly Farm it's scenic as all get out.

COOPER FARM'S STORE

301 West I-45 Fairfield, TX 75840

This is an old-school soda fountain with hundreds of glass bottle sodas and a ton of nostalgic candies to go along with their incredible peaches. This is the type of place that you order the peach milkshake, trust me.

SINCE 1900

619 N. COLORADO

SNOWS BBQ

516 Main St., Lexington, TX 78947

Roughly an hour southeast of Austin, there's nothing like Snows. Did you see the Tootsie Tomantez episode of *Chef's Table*? Your answer tells me what kind of a human you are. When you are in the Barbecue Hall of Fame and have been nominated for two James Beard Awards . . . there's no parallel to what this pitmaster does.

THE SPOETZL BREWERY

603 E Brewery St., Shiner, TX 77984

The Spoetzl Brewery started in 1909 and was originally named "The Shiner Brewing Association," founded by German and Czech immigrants who had settled around the town of Shiner. Unable to find the type of beer they had in their home countries, they decided to brew their own. This is the oldest independent brewery in Texas.

JESTER KING BREWERY

13187 Fitzhugh Rd., Austin, TX 78736

This is a world-renowned maker of farmhouse ales and barrel-aged wild ales, specializing in beers fermented with wild yeast. It's a beautiful property and an amazing place to spend an afternoon.

BARS

BARRELS & AMPS

718 S Austin Ave., Georgetown, TX 78626

NICKEL CITY

1133 E 11th St., Austin, TX 78702

This is an amazing dive bar with amazing cocktails and an even better whiskey selection. It's incredibly well done and it's exciting that the new Nickel City in Fort Worth is scheduled to open soon. My favorite whiskey, the one I bought cases of once I found out they were running low, was a barrel pick from Nickel City. They know their stuff.

PECHE

208 W 4th St., Austin, TX 78701

SEVEN GRAND

405 E 7th St., Austin, TX 78701

Highly recommended. The original Seven Grand is in Los Angeles, but it's sorely lacking in the Texas whiskey section. We enjoy keeping some of those close to home, thank you very much!

AMENDMENT 21

382 Chestnut St., Abilene, TX 79602

BARNETT'S PUBLIC HOUSE

420 Franklin Ave., Waco, TX 76701

The home of the largest whiskey selection in all of Texas. If you can't find it here, odds are our mediocre state government is delaying the distribution of it. And, of course, they'll have more weird Balcones bottles than anywhere else in the state, and rightly so.

ROUGH DRAUGHT

313 Church Ave., College Station, TX 77840

LIQUOR STORES

AUSTIN SHAKER

1199 Airport Blvd., Austin, TX 78702

With multiple locations in Austin, this was the first place to really focus on the cocktail scene and elevate their inventory accordingly. Incredible selection and unbelievably knowledgeable about their products. Their single barrel picks also have a killer reputation.

AUSTIN WINE MERCHANT
512 W 6th St., Austin, TX 78701

OAK LIQUOR CABINET
12636 Research Blvd., Austin, TX 78759

NORMANGEE PACKAGES & GIFTS
108 Main St., Normangee, TX 77871

I was literally trying to avoid construction and found myself at this little package store in the middle of nowhere. The owner has done a wonderful job assembling one of the better Texas whiskey selections in the state. If for any reason you're near, check it out. And for the bourbon hunters out there, the trucks arrive on Thursdays, mid-morning.

THE TEXAS WHISKEY TRAIL

The Texas Whiskey Trail was formally launched at the San Antonio Cocktail Conference in 2019. Currently, there are about twenty members, but that number will certainly increase as additional distillers begin to release their whiskeys. "For about ten years we've been wanting to establish a Texas whiskey trail and to establish certification standards for what defines a Texas whiskey," said Dan Garrison. Joining the organization is free and it's done a great job of gamifying the Texas whiskey experience.

Currently, there are four different trails: North Texas, Hill Country, South Texas, Gulf Coast. What do you expect? Texas is just a little bigger than, say, the distance between Louisville and Lexington. All members of the trail are also members of the Texas Whiskey Association, so you know that anything you buy along the way is made by the most transparent whiskey makers in the state. This is a fantastic way to plot out your trip to come visit Texas, which I know you're already doing. Called it.

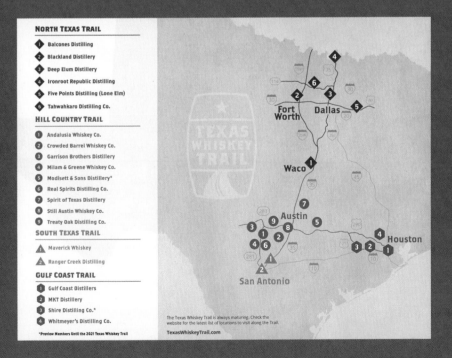

NORTH TEXAS TRAIL

1. Balcones Distilling
2. Blackland Distillery
3. Deep Elum Distillery
4. Ironroot Republic Distilling
5. Five Points Distilling (Lone Elm)
6. Tahwahkaro Distilling Co.

HILL COUNTRY TRAIL

1. Andalusia Whiskey Co.
2. Crowded Barrel Whiskey Co.
3. Garrison Brothers Distillery
4. Milam & Greene Whiskey Co.
5. Modisett & Sons Distillery*
6. Real Spirits Distilling Co.
7. Spirit of Texas Distillery
8. Still Austin Whiskey Co.
9. Treaty Oak Distilling Co.

SOUTH TEXAS TRAIL

△ Maverick Whiskey
△ Ranger Creek Distilling

GULF COAST TRAIL

1. Gulf Coast Distillers
2. MKT Distillery
3. Shire Distilling Co.*
4. Whitmeyer's Distilling Co.

*Preview Members Until the 2021 Texas Whiskey Trail

The Texas Whiskey Trail is always maturing. Check the website for the latest list of locations to visit along the Trail.

TexasWhiskeyTrail.com

HILL COUNTRY AND SOUTH TEXAS

CALAIS WINERY

8115 US-290, Hye, TX 78635

I personally think this is the best wine coming out of Texas. Winemaker Ben Calais is a Frenchman making (but not limited to) fantastic French-style wines.

CHASE'S PLACE

313 E San Antonio St., Fredericksburg, TX 78624

This mid-century era house turned craft cocktail bar and kitchen is one of the highlights of Fredericksburg. Make sure you check out their Hill Country Hipster cocktail, made with Milam & Greene's Rye.

ENCHANTED ROCK STATE PARK

16710 Ranch Rd. 965, Fredericksburg TX

This pink granite mountain is located approximately seventeen miles north of Fredericksburg and twenty-four miles south of Llano. Enchanted Rock covers approximately 640 acres and reaches an elevation of 1,825 feet above sea level. It's super fun for kids to climb on.

GRUENE HALL

1281 Gruene Rd., New Braunfels, TX 78130

This 6,000-square-foot dance hall is the oldest in Texas and it's simultaneously a local music haunt and an internationally recognized, iconic venue. They've hosted the likes of Garth Brooks, Willie Nelson, George Strait, Townes Van Zandt, and launched the careers of Robert Earl Keen, Lucinda Williams, Lyle Lovett, and many more. I saw the Drive-By Truckers here the night I turned forty. That's all I'm at liberty to say about the events of the evening. I don't have to answer your questions. What are you, a cop?

LUCKENBACH TEXAS GENERAL STORE

412 Luckenbach Town Loop, Fredericksburg, TX 78624

Just outside of Fredericksburg, this tiny Hill Country community was established as a trading post in 1849, making it one of the oldest settlements in Gillespie County. Today, you can visit this quaint little Texas town for some live music and a truly Texan experience.

WILLIAM CHRIS VINEYARDS

10352, US-290, Hye, TX 78635

Founded in 2008, this is one of the most scenic wineries in the region, as well as one of the best tasting. It's truly beautiful. And to bring it into the whole whiskey thing, their founder, Chris Brundrett, told me, "We just finished a kickass hot sauce we made in a Garrison Brothers bourbon barrel that had dessert wine in it. Also, Balcones came by and snagged a few dessert wine barrels and we cannot wait to see what they do with them."

SALT LICK BBQ

18300 Farm to Market Rd. 1826, Driftwood, TX 78619

The Salt Lick opened in 1967 and serves some of the most famous BBQ from Texas. The beef ribs are king and one order will find you full as a tick. Fantastic, open air, picnic style, and also cash only and BYOB so prepare yourself accordingly.

RAY'S DRIVE INN

822 SW 19th St., San Antonio, TX 78207

The greatness of the puffy taco must never be questioned. Ray's Drive Inn opened its doors in 1956 and has been serving up this San Antonio classic ever since, doling out an average of 500 puffys a day. If you've never had a puffy taco, you need to remedy this. Go on. I'll wait.

HOTEL EMMA

136 E Grayson St., San Antonio, TX 78215

Once a 19th-century brewhouse, Hotel Emma might be the most beautiful hotel I've ever been to. Full stop. This extraordinary 146-room hotel downtown is also the flagship for the Pearl District, which is easily one of the coolest redevelopments in Texas. They have a killer lobby bar as well (featured in *Texas Cocktails*).

LA PANADERIA

301 E Houston St., San Antonio, TX 78205

Welcome to Bread Cultura! Brothers Jose and David Caceres opened in 2014 as a way for them to show their Mexican heritage to San Antonio. This is an amazing combination of traditional Mexican culinary traditions and a modern, American approach to style and service. Stock up on pan dulce before heading out for your whiskey adventures, because there's nothing better I could think of to soak up booze with.

BARS

BAR 1919

1420 S Alamo St., San Antonio, TX 78204

You will find an unbelievable whiskey selection and some incredible cocktails at this underground bar that was also featured in *Texas Cocktails*. This is where you end your evening in San Antonio, without question.

BRAZED BOURBON & BEER

3709 N St Mary's St., San Antonio, TX 78212

ESQUIRE TAVERN

155 E Commerce St., San Antonio, TX 78205

The Esquire Tavern opened in 1933 to celebrate the end of Prohibition and, excluding five years, has been open ever since. This is one of the first places in San Antonio to focus on cocktails, and the Downstairs at the Esquire is easily one of the most incredible bars in the state. Don't miss this.

LIQUOR STORES

ALAMO CITY LIQUOR

2943 Thousand Oaks, San Antonio, TX 78247

This is a small San Antonio chain with a fabulous selection of all things Texas. Consistently named a top liquor store in the region, with good reason.

GABRIEL'S LIQUOR

1309 North Loop 1604 W, #109, San Antonio, TX 78258

PIG LIQUORS

519 S Presa St., San Antonio, TX 78205

CACTUS LIQUORS

405 S. Highland Ave., Marfa, TX 79843

Yes, I wanted something from Marfa in the book for the cool factor, but also, this is one of the best liquor stores in the state. It's always a delight to be in Marfa and not have to worry about forgetting your essentials. Cactus Liquors has you covered.

GULF COAST

SQUABLE

632 W 19th St., Houston, TX 77008

From the law firm of Heugel and Yu, Squable, in The Heights area of Houston, will serve you one of the most delightful meals you'll ever have. The French cheeseburger, made with raclette, is the stuff that dreams are made of and their cocktail program is exactly as on point as you'd expect from Mr. Heugel.

WEST ALABAMA ICE HOUSE

1919 W Alabama St., Houston, TX 77098

They opened in 1928 as an actual ice house, selling blocks to the surrounding neighborhood. Soon enough, ice wasn't as needed, but a bar sure was. This is a legit Texas honky-tonk, beer joint. Grab a seat at the picnic table and enjoy an ice-cold Texas craft beer and some local country tunes for a fantastic evening.

CRAWFISH & NOODLES

11360 Bellaire Blvd., #990, Houston, TX 77072

Houston is, literally, the most diverse city in the US and home to the largest population of Vietnamese outside of Vietnam. This group of immigrants has created one of the most iconic dishes in Houston, Viet-Cajun crawfish. Coated in garlic butter or tossed in ginger, lemongrass, and scallions, these crawdaddies are archetypal. Crawfish & Noodles has some of the best in town.

BONFIRE GRILL

425 W Main St., Tomball, TX 77375

Tomball isn't usually where you'd think to find one of the coolest whiskey selections in Texas, but Bonfire Grill is absolutely legit. If you're lucky enough to be there for dinner, make sure to end with a Bourbon Flambe Gelato, made with Balcones True Blue 100.

EIGHT ROW FLINT

1039 Yale St., Houston, TX 77008

HOUSTON WATCH COMPANY

913 Franklin St., Houston, TX 77002

KILLEN'S STEAKHOUSE

6425 Broadway St., Pearland, TX 77581

POISON GIRL

641 Westheimer Rd., Suite B, Houston, TX 77006

This is my favorite whiskey bar in Texas. I was introduced to Poison Girl during the cocktail book as "the place you end up at the end of the evening" from the majority of bartenders in Houston whom I talked to. Unreal whiskey selection in a legit dive bar. Poison Girl is a gem. Make sure to check out their barrel picks because they have some genuinely unique whiskeys.

RESERVE 101

1201 Caroline St., Suite 100, Houston, TX 77002

I'd say this is the crown jewel of Houston whiskey bars. Mike Raymond has always done an incredible job of keeping up with the greatest whiskeys available and his collaborations with the Houston Whiskey Social are stuff of legend. Reserve 101 should be at the top of your Houston to-do list.

ROSEWATER

1606 Clear Lake City Blvd., Houston, TX 77062

LIQUOR STORES

CARNEY LIQUOR

2174 Spring Stuebner Rd., Suite 350, Spring, TX 77389

DANDY LIQUOR

25681 Nelson Way #140, Katy, TX 77494

VILLAGE LIQUOR

3406 N Shepherd Dr., Houston, TX 77018

This four-store, Houston-based chain has a fabulous array of Texas whiskey and is always doing barrel picks with Texas distillers. Their Cask Strength True Blue pick from Balcones was a personal favorite. Make sure you ask to see what they have currently.

HOUSTON WINE MERCHANT

2646 S Shepherd Dr., Houston, TX 77098

LONGHORN LIQUOR BEER & WINE

3939 Dowlen Road Suite #12, Beaumont, TX 77706

LY'S LIQUOR

3914 Navigation Blvd., Houston, TX 77003

RICE FINE WINE & LIQUOR

5108 Spruce St., Bellaire, TX 77401

All you need to do is follow Rice Fine Wine & Liquor on social media to know what incredible barrel selections they're currently stocking. Wonderfully knowledgeable staff and a great vibe as soon as you walk in the door.

RYAN'S LIQUOR

265 Cypresswood Dr., Spring, TX 77388

There are literally bottles of Balcones here that are not available anywhere else. Ryan's is a fantastic store and they know their stuff when it comes to Texas whiskey. Definitely a place to do a little bourbon hunting. But everyone knows that so... maybe not. Regardless, amazing selection.

TONY K'S HOME OF FINE SPIRITS

2720 Bissonnet St., Houston, TX 77005

IMAGE CREDITS

John Whalen: Pages 2, 3, 6, 7, 8, 9, 12, 16, 17, 22, 23, 25, 26, 28, 29, 32, 33, 37, 38, 39, 42, 43, 48, 50, 51, 56, 57, 58, 62, 65, 69, 70, 71, 74, 75, 81, 92, 93, 99, 110, 111, 112, 116, 120, 121, 129, 130, 131, 135, 137, 138. 140, 141, 142, 145, 147, 148, 154, 156, 157, 159, 160, 161, 163, 164, 165, 167, 168, 171, 172, 180, 187, 196, 197, 208, 212, 214, 215, 216, 217, 223, 224, 233, 235, 236, 237, 239, 240, 249, 250, 251, 253, 254, 255, 256, 259, 262, 263, 265, 275 (bottom), 278, 299, 301, 302, 303, 305, 320, 321, 322, 325, 326, 327, 329, 330, 331, 333, 338, 339, 344, 347, 349, 354, 359, 364, 365, 372, 373, 376, 383, 389, 390. 393, 398, 401, 402, 405, 406, 407, 409, 412, 413 (top), 414, 415, 416, 419, 420, 421, 423, 425, 427, 428, 431, 432, 434, 437, 438, 440, 441, 443, 444, 446, 447, 452, 453, 454, 457, 458, 459, 463, 464, 465, 474, 475, 476, 477, 480, 486 (top), 488, 489

Shutterstock: Pages 4, 5, 10, 20, 21, 44, 45, 46, 178, 179, 247, 270, 271, 272, 396, 397, 472, 473, 479, 483, 486 (bottom), 491, 492, 494, 496, 499, 500, 501, 503, 510, 511

Library of Congress: Pages 72, 242

Nico Martini: Page 107

All other images courtesy of the respective distilleries.

ACKNOWLEDGMENTS

It's not often that you do something that impacts your legacy in the way a project like this does. I'm grateful for the opportunity to tell the first portion of the very long tale of whiskey in Texas, and I sincerely hope I've done it justice. I know this story is bigger than the one who's telling it, but I'm blessed to be that man. I could not be more proud of the entire Texas whiskey industry.

Above all else, this book is dedicated to my sons and their beautiful mother. Declan, you are so much like me and the light you bring to my life will never dim. Beckett, I have fallen in love with your words and your heart. You've taught me to be extra brave and I can only hope I do the same for you. Sarah, you are the reason any of this is possible. You are my favorite adventure. I will love you for always.

Sincere thank you to everyone who helped make this possible. John Whalen and the rest of the team at Cider Mill Press, thank you for believing in my ability to pull this off. I'm pretty happy with it and frankly, no take backs. Thank you to all of those in the Texas whiskey family whose stories I've tried to tell. Thank you to the distillers willing to take risks, to the farmers who are willing to grow creatively, to the other storytellers who are screaming from the hilltops that Texas whiskey is special. Thank you to the people who are willing to taste whiskey like they've never had before and not discount it because it's a bit unfamiliar.

To my mom and dad, thank you for always letting me figure it out on my own and letting me find my own voice. To the squad, I'll see you at the Hitchcock. To Mad Mike, you owe me $50. A huge thank you to all of those who've come along this whiskey journey with me, this is just the beginning. To the Whiskey Exchange and all that entails, thank you for your generosity.

In Texas, the pride in our state can only be outdone by our hunger to prove why it's the best. We have a certain swagger, but that just because we're right. Texans... we may be full of shit, but at least we know it don't stink. If you bought this book because you love Texas whiskey, thank you. If you bought this book because you doubt Texas whiskey, buckle up.

Texas Forever.

ABOUT THE AUTHOR

NICO MARTINI lives in Dallas, Texas, with his wife, Sarah, and sons Beckett and Declan. His first book, *Texas Cocktails* (Cider Mill Press) was released in 2018. Martini is the co-founder of Grayson Whiskey. He's a former guest lecturer at The University of Texas at Dallas, the co-founder of Bar Draught, and has presented seminars for Bar Institute, San Antonio Cocktail Conference, and Portland Cocktail Week. In various former lives, Martini was the program director and on-air for CBS Radio's The Indieverse 100.3 HD2 in Dallas, has been on tour with hippie jugglers, used to perform in Wild West comedy gunfight shows, and is a member of the Lincoln Center Director's Lab. He received, but didn't accept, a hockey scholarship to Penn State and recently gave a TEDx talk on cocktails. He's also the biggest Texas whiskey apologist you've ever met and encourages you to visit texaswhiskeybook.com for proof.

ABOUT CIDER MILL PRESS BOOK PUBLISHERS

Good ideas ripen with time. From seed to harvest, Cider Mill Press brings fine reading, information, and entertainment together between the covers of its creatively crafted books. Our Cider Mill bears fruit twice a year, publishing a new crop of titles each spring and fall.

"Where Good Books Are Ready for Press"

VISIT US ONLINE AT
cidermillpress.com

OR WRITE TO US AT
PO Box 454
12 Spring St.
Kennebunkport, Maine 04046

Joya de Ceboleta
Joyita
Sabino
Parida
Socorro

Don Pedro
alverde
Cristobal

Mal Pais Spr.

Ft Stanton

N E W

Y O U N G

LLANO ESTACADO
OR TERRITORY
STAKED PLAIN

Extensive Table Lands
elevated some 2400 ft. above
the Ocean and destitute of
both Wood and Water

Rio Pecos

R. Bonito

M E X I C O

Rio Feliz

Venando Spr.

R. Penasco

Sulphur Spring

North Fork

Double Mount

a Ana
Sierra
Hueco
Ft Fillmore
Mesilla

Los Cornudos
Ojos de los
Alamos

R. Santos
Savin Gr.

Sandy Country with
course grass, but no water

Big
Spring

Ft Chadbo

Frontera
anklin
Magoffinsville
Isleta
Socorro
San Elizario
San Ignacio

Hueco Pass

Salt
Spring

Delaware Cr.

Guadalupe
Mts.

Guadalupe Pass

B E X A R

Twin Mts.

North Fork

Red Fo

Concho

Guadalupe

E L   P A S O

Presidio Mts.

Presidio Pass

RIO PECOS

Horse Head
Crossing

Lipan R.

Good Spr. R.

Boiling Fork R.

Spr

Ft S.

Laguna de Patos

RIO GRANDE

Eagle
Spr.

Toyah Cr.

Leon Spr.

Head of
Limpia

Spr.

Ft Davis

Escondido
Spr. & Cr.

Comanche Spr.

T E R R I T O R Y

R. Carmen

P R E S I D I O

RIO PECOS

Lagunas

M

High Mountain
Ranges

Presidio del Norte

Fort Leaton

E

Rio Conchos

X

Presidio de
San Vicente

2nd Crossing

R. San Pedro

Ft Clark

RIO GRANDE

I

Falls of
Presidio
del R. Grande

GALVESTON BAY,
AND
VICINITY.
42

HARRIS CO.

Clear L.

Clear Cr.

Dickerson B.

Taylors

San Jacinto River

Cedar B.

Turtle
Bay

Mouths
of
Trinity R.

North Pt.

GALVESTON

Clear Cr.

Double B.

BRAZORIA

Mustang B.

Choco

Chocolate Bay

Highland B.

Central

COUNTY

R. R.

COUNTY

Edwards Pt.

Fish Pt.

Dickerson
Bayou

Moses
L.

Dollar Pt.

Smith
Pt.

Hannas
Reef

Stevenson's Pt.

CHAMBERS CO.

East Bay

East Bay B.

Halls

Pelican

West Bay

Inter

Eagle
Gro

G A L V E S T O N   B A Y

Bolivar Pt. & Lt Ho.

Bird Key

Fort Pt.

Bolivar Peninsula

Muscle

Gal

G A L V E S T O N   Id.